The Fourth Gate
(A negyedik kapu)

by Péter Kárpáti
translated by Dennis Kelly
from a literal translation by Ildikó Noémi Nagy
and Katalin Trencsényi

The Fourth Gate was first read in the UK, in this translation, at the Cottesloe Theatre on 18 June 2004.

The reading was directed by Alex Murdoch.

ALRA
www.alra.co.uk

CHANNELS

By Philippe Le Moine, International Projects Manager NT Studio

One of the National Theatre Studio's flagship initiatives, *CHANNELS* aims to instigate and nurture a direct creative exchange between the vibrant, but somewhat insular, world of British theatre and its corresponding foreign counterparts.

A programme with ever-expanding horizons, each *CHANNELS* project strives to bring together writers, translators and directors from the UK and one specific country, with a view to translating and presenting a selection of current British plays abroad, and foreign works at the National and beyond.

At the heart of the project lies a process of hand-in-hand interaction, with the playwright and translator taking a literal translation as their starting point and building a mutual understanding of one another's methods and ideas. These 'residencies' are the cornerstone of a scheme infused with discovery and exchange.

Five French plays were translated, read at the National Theatre and published by Oberon Books in 2002. *Channels (Hungary)* is the second project and runs alongside *Channels (Argentina)*. Quebec and The Czech Republic are also on the cards.

Following the heartening success of *CHANNELS*, a network of like-minded organisations has emerged. INTERTEXT covers major partner languages: French, German and Italian, and carries forward the spirit of *CHANNELS* as a permanent European platform for translation and encounters.

For more information on the NT Studio's International projects:
studio@nationaltheatre.org.uk

NT Studio

Head of Studio	LUCY DAVIES
International Projects Manager	PHILIPPE LE MOINE
Studio Manager	NATASHA BUCKNOR
Technical Manager	EDDIE KEOGH
Studio Administrator	RACHEL LONERGAN
Studio Assistant	MATTHEW POXON
Book Keeper	VERA PROLE
Reception	CATHY MILLER, JANLYN BALES
Security Officer	LLOYD WILDMAN

NT Literary Department

Literary Manager	JACK BRADLEY
Assistant Literary Manager	LAURA GRIBBLE
Senior Reader	CHRIS CAMPBELL
Scripts Assistant	SARAH CLARKE

CHANNELS (Hungary)

by Katalin Trencsényi

When I was a teenager I came across an interesting riddle about reading. It concerned two brothers who were trying to read a book. One of them could recognise the letters and read aloud the words without understanding the meaning, whereas the other could understand the meaning, but could not interpret the letters. So they decided to work together. The one who knew the letters spelt them out, and the other explained the meaning of the words. The question was: which of them was reading? The answer was neither of them. Both of these skills are needed in order to read a text.

This story occurred to me several times whilst working with the British playwrights on their English translations of these four plays for the *Channels (Hungary)* project. Sometimes it seemed as if we were trying to make the impossible possible. How could we two translators – one who could not read the play in its original language and one whose mother tongue wasn't English – work together on one piece?

We had the original play in Hungarian, and a literal translation with a number of added footnotes clarifying problematic areas. This formed the basis for several drafts which were worked and reworked to arrive at the final version of the translation.

Like the two brothers in the riddle we couldn't have done it without each other. We literal translators knew the language and the cultural background of the play – where the play 'came from'. Whereas our British playwright colleagues knew the language and the theatrical culture into which the play was heading.

During our one-week residency at the National Theatre Studio we 'twins' became 'triplets', as the Hungarian playwrights joined us to help with the translation. They answered questions we had about the plays, explained hidden meanings, tiny details and revealed their way of thinking and their working process. We went through the plays word-by-word, comparing the translations with the original, checking things like the social context, the rhythms of the phrases, and debating the precise meaning of certain words.

We had to answer such questions as: How many miles from Budapest is Irgács, the hidden village where Zoltán Egressy's play is set? Would a Hassidic Jew use the word synagogue? How should we distinguish formal and informal verb conjugations in English? What kind of drug are the gangsters dealing in Ákos Németh's play? What's the English equivalent for 'pálinka'?

As one of the playwrights, Péter Kárpáti recalled *"A painstaking but very exciting process now began: we were flying from word to word! ... Dennis [Kelly] enjoyed the excess and the 'garlic-spiced' humour of the Hungarian text – I enjoyed his elegance, the way he delicately sharpened the Hungarian sentences: in English they sound less ambiguous, more precise. I can hardly speak any English, he doesn't speak Hungarian, but strangely our intuitive sense of language enabled us to engage in an elaborate dialogue. Who can explain this?"*

Our work did not conclude with the end of the residency. We spent another five months finalising, checking, clarifying and double-checking the translations.

This isn't to say that using a single translator isn't effective, and often even preferable. But using multiple translators suited the nature of this project.

Aside from producing good English translations of the plays, the other aim of the project was to encourage the playwrights to exchange ideas and perhaps learn from each other; maybe in the process discovering new worlds, different ways of thinking, fresh working methods. Perhaps it also showed that regardless of where in this world a playwright is working he/she will face similar questions and problems. As a discussion during the residency revealed, whether Hungarian or English, it is impossible to find inspiration when writing with a blue biro!

The Fourth Gate by Péter Kárpáti is based on a collection of Hassidic stories. Hassidism, a Jewish 'folk' movement, was founded in the mid-eighteenth century by the healer, Baal Shem Tov who was born in Podolia (today's Ukraine). This charismatic leader attracted a wide following throughout Eastern-Europe and his teachings encouraged people to worship God and keep his commandments in a simple, joyful way. Hassidism talks about personal rather than national redemption and it emphasises that God is to be found in every aspect of life.

Thus according to the Hassidic view everything can be sacred: eating, singing, dancing, trading, love making, not to mention storytelling. And it is storytelling that the Hassids were really famous for. This is where Kárpáti comes in. He takes as his starting point the stories collected by Jiři Langer of this once thriving Hassidic community and fashions from them a beautiful patchwork.

At the centre of *The Fourth Gate* is the story of Urele and his quest through these Hassidic communities to find his Teacher or Master. Each scene revolves around an encounter with a famous rabbi and the adventures which ensue. Urele learns something from each of them and each adventure is a step towards his personal 'enlightenment'.

Kárpáti's play can be located within the European tradition of *Bildungsromans* (e.g.: *Wilhelm Meister's Apprenticeship* by Goethe). However it could also be seen as a fairytale in which the hero has to undergo different challenges in order to develop, and where at the end he returns home as a wiser person.

The original Hassidic storytellers themselves appear as the narrators in *The Fourth Gate*; we learn the story of Urele from them. They tell it, enact it, and sometimes comment on it. They contribute to each other's stories and sometimes stop for a while to sing their favourite song. The play ends with them lying together under the Sukka (a special tent built for the Harvest Festival), "*sleeping or staring at the sky*", enjoying the last moments of being one with the universe, of being part of a community.

So when are these stories being told? Let Kárpáti answer this question: *"The play is set in the twilight years of the Eastern Hassidic community, but when their way of life still existed. This was before World War One, and the destruction of the old world and the old ways . It is set perhaps in the community of Belz... maybe on the last night, before they have to leave the village... it is September 1907, during their Harvest Festival. They all know that they won't be spending the next Harvest Festival together. One of them will be in America, another will go to be an accountant in Lemberg..."*

So is the play a Jewish Decameron for the twentieth century? It is more than that. *The Fourth Gate* also deals with our own personal search for knowledge and spiritual growth. As Kárpáti notes: *"We spend a long time seeking our master (a wise mentor), until one day we realise with a surprise that others regard us to be their master. – Have we really become a 'master' during the search? I don't think so, but we have grown old – that is for sure."*

All four of the plays in this anthology are new dramas written by the best contemporary Hungarian playwrights of the new generation. Tried, tested and awarded in Hungary and on the continent. The world they describe may be a little different, but you might find the people they introduce surprisingly familiar.

Special thanks to my husband Nick Tomalin, for his help with the translations, Vivienne Menkes-Ivry a great friend, for her wise advice and encouragement and to Rachel Grunwald and Esther and Winston Held for their expertise in Hassidic matters.

PÉTER KÁRPÁTI

Péter Kárpáti is an award-winning playwright and dramaturg. His plays are performed in mainstream theatres in Hungary and also on the radio. Two of them have also been made into films. Three volumes of his plays have been published in Hungary, in 1992, 1995 and 1999, and his work has been translated into Finnish, German, Polish and several other languages, including English. In 1996 Nick Hern Books published his *Everywoman* in an anthology of Hungarian plays and this translation was performed in London at the Baron's Court Theatre in 2002.

DENNIS KELLY

Dennis Kelly studied Drama and Theatre Arts at Goldsmiths, graduating in 2001. Plays are: *Whitepig* (Soho Theatre 2002, reading), *Debris* (Latchmere Theatre 2003, BAC 2004, Burgtheater, Vienna 2004), *Blackout* (Soho Theatre Writers' Festival and WCMD, 2003), *The Colony* (The Wire, Radio 3 2004) and *Osama the Hero* (Paines Plough Wild Lunch, 2004). *Debris* is about to be translated into Italian for the Quartieri dell'Arte in Rome as part of the Intertext project.

ILDIKÓ NOÉMI NAGY

Ildikó Noémi Nagy was born in Canada but has been living in Hungary since 1993. In 1997 she obtained a degree as a viola player from the teachers' training college run by the Liszt Ferenc Music Academy in Budapest, and in 2002 was awarded an MA in American literature at the Eötvös Loránd University, also in Budapest. She works as a freelance translator of literary texts, and books on film, music and art. Her translation of László Garaczi's novel *Lemur, Who Are You?* was launched in Glasgow in August 2003 as part of the preliminary programme for Magyar Magic – Hungary in Focus 2004.

KATALIN TRENCSÉNYI

Katalin Trencsényi was trained as a dramaturg in Hungary and is a founder member of the Dramaturgs' Network in Britain, where she has been living since 2001. She has worked for the Central School of Speech and Drama, the Courtyard Theatre and the Royal Academy of Dramatic Art. As a member of the Young Vic's Young Directors' Forum, she sometimes exchanges the dramaturg's stool for the director's chair: in 2000 she directed a season of staged readings of Hungarian contemporary plays at the Hungarian Cultural Centre; and her most recent work as a director was at the Young Vic Studio, as part of the "On War" project. She has also had a book published on theatre with people with Down's Syndrome.

CHANNELS (Hungary) 2004
National Theatre, Cottesloe

Thursday 17 June, 2.30pm
THE STONEWATCHER
by János Háy
translated by Phil Porter
directed by Anna Mackmin

Friday 18 June, 2.30pm
THE FOURTH GATE
by Péter Kárpáti
translated by Dennis Kelly
directed by Alex Murdoch

Thursday 24 June, 2.30pm
CAR THIEVES
by Ákos Németh
translated by Ché Walker
directed by Ché Walker

Friday 25 June, 2.30pm
PORTUGAL
by Zoltán Egressy
translated by Ryan Craig
directed by Matt Wilde

MAGYAR MAGIC – Hungary in Focus 2004, a year-long celebration of Hungarian art and talent in the UK

by Katalin Bogyay, Director of the Hungarian Cultural Centre and Magyar Magic

Culture is us, it is democratic, it is about experiences and relationships. For me, culture is a framework for collective creativity.

I had a dream four years ago. To create a Hungarian Cultural Centre, a cultural space in London that would provide an important meeting-place where ideas, talent and experiences from both East and West could be exchanged in an inspirational and welcoming environment. Four years on, people and cultures from the Thames to the Danube have indeed come together in Maiden Lane to take part in our cultural exchange. A network of artists, writers, musicians and intellectuals has evolved organically, watched over by the spirits of the Vaudeville Theatre, which gives the HCC a home in Covent Garden. Our culture is welcoming and inclusive, facilitating creative links and finding meeting-points. These aspirations are symbolized by the Centre's Palladian window, which is always open.

Now, on the threshold of the New Europe, within the framework of Magyar Magic, we will share with you, in a very intense way, our thousand-year-old cultural heritage, which is full of unique, high-level but often lesser-known artistic values, and also full of glamour and good-tempered fun. Hungarian culture is a wonderful mixture of traditional, organic and contemporary elements.

As members of Europe, we are all in a position to absorb, peacefully and of our own free will, one another's cultural influences. And let us hope that out of this melting pot a New European style will emerge, which will in no way diminish the cultural identities of individual nations. I see Magyar Magic as the beginning of a new kind of cultural dialogue that will continue far into the future.

Thank you to everyone for believing in my vision of four years ago and for joining me on this journey.

Thanks are due to the Ministry of Cultural Heritage in Hungary for its support and its determination to see Hungarian Cultural Seasons launched all over Europe.

Thank you to my dedicated colleagues at the HCC, whose boundless energy, knowledge and team spirit have helped me to make this dream come true.

Thanks, too, go to our partners and friends here in the UK whom I proudly regard as 'Honorary Hungarians'.

This book is published as part of Magyar Magic – Hungary in Focus 2004, a year-long celebration of Hungarian art and talent in the United Kingdom supported by the Hungarian Ministry of Cultural Heritage.

www.magyarmagic.com

NEMZETI KULTURÁLIS ÖRÖKSÉG
MINISZTÉRIUMA

THE NATIONAL THEATRE

The National Theatre presents an eclectic mix of new plays and classics, with seven or eight productions in repertory at any one time. It aims constantly to re-energise the great traditions of the British stage and to expand the horizons of audiences and artists alike, and aspires to reflect in its repertoire the diversity of the culture. At its Studio, the National offers a space for research and development for the NT's stages and the theatre as a whole. Through the NT Education Department, tomorrow's audiences are addressed. Through an extensive programme of Platform performances, backstage tours, foyer music, exhibitions, and free outdoor entertainment the National recognises that the theatre doesn't begin and end with the rise and fall of the curtain.

NT Platforms are daytime and early-evening discussions, talks and interviews offering an insight into the National's current productions and showcasing theatre-related events.

National Theatre, South Bank, London SE1 9PX
www.nationaltheatre.org.uk
Registered Charity No: 224223

Royal National Theatre

THE FOURTH GATE

A Klezmer Play

"Actually," said wise Reb Nahman of Bratslav, "we spend our whole lives in a magical dream. We only return back to our true selves from this dream if someone tells us stories of the saints."

First published in 2004 by Oberon Books Ltd
(Incorporating Absolute Classics.)
521 Caledonian Road, London N7 9RH
Tel: 020 7607 3637 / Fax: 020 7607 3629
e-mail: oberon.books@btinternet.com
www.oberonbooks.com

A catalogue record for this book is available from the British
Library.

ISBN: 1 84002 468 2

Printed in Great Britain by Antony Rowe Ltd, Chippenham.

Characters

The Hassids (the storytellers)

AVRUMENKO

MOYSHELE

SARAH

THE GIRL

The Saints

HOLY REB URELE, the Seraph

YUDE HERSH, the shochet

and

HOLY REBE REB ELIMELECH

HOLY REB YEYBE

THE HOLY CHOCHEM, the Wisest of the Wise

AARON, the Messiah

ZISHE, the fool of God

REB SHLOYMELE, The Master

Five or six actors (though it can be more) play all of the characters reflecting the Hassidic passion for storytelling depicted in *The Nine Gates.*

The musicians:

KING DAVID, the band leader (first violin)

And the FOREFATHERS, a Klezmer Band

PRONUNCIATION GUIDE

For reasons of space we cannot give the pronunciation of all the foreign words which occur in the play, so this is just a guide to the most often used words.

Most of the foreign words in the play are Yiddish. For further information on pronunciation contact YIVO (Yiddish Institute for Jewish Research).

However for the pronunciation of the Yiddish words there are a few general rules which may help you:

ey	as in the English hey
ay	as in the English sky
i	as in the English ski
e	as in the English hen
tsh	as in the English match
ch	guttural h, similar to an emphatic yuck! (in our pronunciation guide it is signalled with 'H')

Below find a guide to the standard Yiddish pronunciation.

Avrumenko	[avroohmenko]
Baal Shem Tov	[bhaal shem tov]
batlan	[bhatln]
Belz	[beltz]
Bereshit	[bereyshis]
bocher	[boHer] (very short)
Chochem	[HoHm]
Eliezer	[eleeyehzer]
Elimelech	[eyhlimeyhleH]
etrog	[esreg]
Fraidele	[fraydehleh]
Hedad!	[hedad]
káva (Czech)	[cahvah]
Koritz	[korits]
Lay'day nokelach,	
ungeschmoltsen, ach.	[lei'dei nokelaH oongheshmoltsen aH]
lechaim	[leHaym]
lulav	[loohlev]
Lysychansk	[lizjhensk]
Maggid	[mhagheed]
Malakhha-mavet	[maleH hah-moves]
Mazel tov!	[mazl tov]
Menachem Mendel	[menaHm mendl]
Mezhirech	[mezheerech]
mohel	[moyhl]
Moyshele	[moysheleh] (accent heavily on first syllable)
Nagykálló (Hungarian)	[nadjkhalloh]
nebechel	[nebeHl]
Ostroh	[ostroh]
Purim	[poorim]
Rambam	[rhambham]
Reb	[reb]
Rebe	[rebbe]
Shlomo	[shloymeh]

Shalom Aleichem	[sholm aleyHem]
Shiye	[sheeyeh]
Shloymele	[shloymehleh] (accent heavily on first syllable)
Shochet	[shoyHt]
Simche Binem	[seemHeh bheenhem]
Sulchan Arukh	[shulHn oruH]
Tishri	[tishri]
Yeybe	[yebeh]
Yitzhak Eyzik Toub	[yeetzHok ayzik toub]
Yoynisn Aybeshitz	[yoineeshn aibshitz]
Yude Hersh	[yeedeh hersh]
Zishe	[zjheesheh]

The extraordinary world of the now extinct Hassidic Empire shines out through The Nine Gates *by Jiři Langer of Prague. This is my attempt to capture a brilliant ray of light. Special thanks to Péter Forgács for introducing me to* The Nine Gates.

PART ONE

1
(Holy Little Reb Urele)

*Music. A man sits by the side of the road, crying. A cart is rushing
through the night, the occupants sing at the top of their lungs:*

Avrumenko, Avrumenko,
Nasz stary tatenko,
Czemu nie nadchodzisz,
Czemu ty nie prosisz
Pana Boga za nas, Pana Boga za nas?
Zeby Bes-hamikdos nam zbudowali
Nasze dzieci in der Toire w'yraz Shomayim wychowali –

AVRUMENKO: Help me! For the love of God, help me.

MOYSHELE: What's the matter? What are you crying for?

FATHER: Why shouldn't I cry? I have a son born; already
eight days old! Eight days old and not yet circumcised.

MOYSHELE: What? What's the matter with you? He has to
be circumcised within eight days!

AVRUMENKO: Haven't you got a mohel in your village?

FATHER: A mohel? We haven't even got a *Jew.* I need ten
Jews to pray at his circumcision. If I had money I could
ship ten Jews in from the city: How can I afford ten
Jews? I couldn't even pay their travel.

He cries.

MOYSHELE: Why don't *you* go to the city?

AVRUMENKO: Good idea. Go see those wealthy Jews in
the city.

15

FATHER: Too late. Look at the sky. See that star going down on the horizon?

MOYSHELE: Oy veh! That was the eighth day?

FATHER: We came out here this morning with my little baby Urele, hoping a cart would come this way and take us to the city, or maybe that God in his infinite wisdom would perform a miracle and send us an entire Jewish community – but nothing. We've been sitting here, crying since morning: nothing. No carts, no Jews, no –

He notices they are laughing.

You think this is funny?

AVRUMENKO: You are a lucky man!

Long pause.

We are Jews!

MOYSHELE: We are exactly ten.

AVRUMENKO: We have a Rabbi among us too. (*Indicating MOYSHELE.*) Moyshele!

MOYSHELE: (*Indicating AVRUMENKO.*) We have a mohel…

AVRUMENKO: And we have a *very* sharp knife!

MOYSHELE: We even have a band who will play at the ceremony…

AVRUMENKO: And afterwards we will dance and have a big holy party!

MOYSHELE: Not just any old wandering ragamuffin musicians, these boys.

AVRUMENKO: Play, David!

MOYSHELE: And we have so much food…

AVRUMENKO: We even have vodka. Aaron, crack open the vodka! Give the poor man a drink!

MOYSHELE: You've had enough, Avrumenko! And stop waving that knife around. I want you to cut this boy's holy penis properly, so that not a single drop more blood is shed than is absolutely necessary. It is incredibly precious; the blood of this boy was brewed at the beginning of time.

Music.

Jicchok, Jicchoknyenku,
Nasz stary tatenko,
Czemu nie nadchodzisz,
Czemu ty nie prosisz
Pana Boga za nas, Pana Boga za nas?
Zeby Bes-hamikdos nam zbudowali
Nasze dzieci in der Toire w'yraz Shomayim wychowali –

Sound of a baby, crying.

SARAH: This is how the little holy Reb Urele comes into this world, may the light of his merits protect us. The circumcision that night was more spectacular that anything seen or heard since The Creation itself.

And then the guests depart. They were never, ever seen again. Who were they? King David leads the orchestra...

Flourish from the band. DAVID comes forward and bows.

SARAH: Moses is the Rabbi...

Flourish. MOYSHELE comes forward and bows.

THE GIRL: Our Father Abraham holds the knife and the prophet Elijah dances...

Flourish. AVRUMENKO comes forward and bows. He makes the fur coat of Elijah that he uses later in the scene bow as well.

MOYSHELE: And it's the high priest Aaron who cracks open the vodka…

Flourish. AARON comes forward and bows.

AVRUMENKO: And Sarah, Mother of the Jews changes holy Little Reb Urele into a nice clean nappy.

Flourish. SARAH comes forward and bows.

THE GIRL: When the Messiah comes, we'll see them all again. But until that moment comes, we'll sing…

They sing.

SARAH & THE GIRL: Moyshe, reio meheimo nas. Moyshe, reio meheimo nas.

AVRUMENKO & MOYSHELE: Moses, our faithful shepherd…

SARAH & THE GIRL: Czemu nie nadchodzisz?

AVRUMENKO & MOYSHELE: Why do you not come…

SARAH & THE GIRL: Czemu ty nie prosisz?

AVRUMENKO & MOYSHELE: Why do you not pray…

SARAH & THE GIRL: Pana Boga za nas, Pana Boga za nas,

AVRUMENKO & MOYSHELE: To the Lord for us…

SARAH & THE GIRL: Zeby Bes-hamikdos nam zbudowali…

AVRUMENKO & MOYSHELE: To re-build our Temple…

SARAH & THE GIRL: Nasze dzieci in der Torie…

AVRUMENKO & MOYSHELE: To bring up our children in the Law…

SARAH & THE GIRL: W'yraz Shomayim wychowali…

AVRUMENKO & MOYSHELE: …and the fear of God.

SARAH & THE GIRL: L'arczeini, nas zaprovaditi…

AVRUMENKO & MOYSHELE: …Return us to our land…

SARAH & THE GIRL: L'arczeini, nas. L'arczeini, nas.

SARAH: On the third birthday of holy Reb Urele, they cut his hair…

AVRUMENKO: They even shave his head…

MOYSHELE: Preserving his little side-locks, of course…

SARAH: … they bath him, dress him in a festive caftan, and hang an enormous golden chain around his little neck that has been leant to them by the wife of their landlord.

MOYSHELE: An enormous gold chain, which is, perhaps, a little too enormous as he can hardly stand.

SARAH: And then they put holy little Reb Urele on top of the table, and place on his head, not his father's black velvet hat, as is usual on such occasions…

AVRUMENKO: … but a magnificent fur shtreimel …

SARAH: …the kind that only saints and famous rabbis wear.

AVRUMENKO: It's time for holy little Reb Urele to deliver his sermon on the table.

SARAH: His parents didn't have money for sweets, but holy little Reb Urele's birthday still turned out to be a great day. Urele did not give his sermon on the table like other three year-old children, who say... 'I em a leetle snake who alweys sez taki' –

AVRUMENKO: Holy Reb Urele gave the sermon like a –

SARAH: – like a real alefbes kind!

MOYSHELE: The cleverest kid in the class!

SARAH: Like a chochem attik!

AVRUMENKO: A great scholar!

SARAH: Like an etzesgeber!

MOYSHELE: Someone who understands the entire world!

SARAH: Like Rambam!

AVRUMENKO: A philosopher of extraordinary vision!

SARAH: Like a true goylem aylem!

MOYSHELE: Like a... true... goylem aylem!

Little URELE is on the table. Pause.

URELE: (*Demonstrating.*) We hold the cup in our right hand, pass it from our right hand to our left hand, and pour half of the water with our left hand onto our right hand (like so...). Then we take the cup in our right hand and pour the other half of the water with our right hand over our left hand. We rub our hands together. We give thanks to our Lord God for making us holy and for teaching us to wash our hands. Then we dry our hands. When we dry, our left hand must be covered by the towel. This is very important, yet still it gets forgotten! There are great and sublime secrets in the cleansing of the hands. If our hands are perfectly dried then finally we can eat the food –

ALL: *(Clapping and yelling.)* Mazel tov! Gitz gepoylt!

Music. They are about to tuck into the food, but URELE stops them with a gesture. Music waits.

URELE: And…

Pause. They wait.

on Sunday we eat kartoflyes…

AVRUMENKO: Potatoes.

URELE: …on Monday we eat zhemakes…

SARAH: Potatoes.

URELE: …Tuesday we have erdepl…

MOYSHELE: Potatoes.

URELE: …Wednesday we have bulbes…

AVRUMENKO: Spuds.

URELE: …Thursday we have barbulyes…

SARAH: Potatoes.

URELE: …on Friday we have krumpirn…

MOYSHELE: Yes.

URELE: …and on the holy Sabbath we get…

ALL: …potato-kugel!

URELE: On Purim and birthdays we get kreplach filled with curd. If you have never eaten kreplach, you've never lived. Let me tell you there is a mystical meaning to be found in the eating of kreplach – but this knowledge is the preserve of the saints.

He sits down on the table, eats an oversize kreplach. Pause.

SARAH: Urele's wife was called Fraidele. Patient, faithful, humble –

AVRUMENKO: A real hassidatzke yidene!

MOYSHELE: Fraidele toiled as a servant, so that her husband would be free to study the Talmud all day.

SARAH: Later she opened up a department store in the cellar of their house.

This shop is incredible – anything can be bought here, the entire world and all of its contents seem to lying on the shelves. Except what it is that you're actually looking for.

MOYSHELE: In one corner customers can see a pathetic creature, stinking from starvation and poverty, dressed in pitiful rags stooping over the Talmud.

AVRUMENKO: And in the other they find Fraidele, fluttering happily behind the counter because she knows that she will be rewarded in heaven for all her 'I'm afraid we're out of that's. She will sit at golden tables with her husband and converse with saints and prophets and wise men.

MOYSHELE: Then one day, Elijah himself –

AVRUMENKO: – Yes, the Prophet Elijah himself stepped through the door and into the shop.

AVRUMENKO puts on the fur hat and fur coat of a Polish peasant and opens the door, ringing the bell.

ELIJAH (AVRUMENKO.): Got any rope?

FRAIDELE (SARAH.): What kind of rope?

ELIJAH: Hemp rope, thick as my finger.

URELE: I'm afraid we're out of tha –

FRAIDELE: Here we are; hemp rope, thick as your finger.

ELIJAH: How much?

FRAIDELE: What?

ELIJAH: What is the price?

She looks at URELE.

FRAIDELE: S... six?

ELIJAH: Six?

FRAIDELE: Five.

ELIJAH: Five? So cheap?

FRAIDELE: Cheap?

URELE: You think that's cheap? That's not cheap? You should go across the road to the Cripple Vuvche's. Half the price.

ELIJAH: Yes, yes, fine: but it is not the same quality.

URELE: What? No quality at Vuvche's? *This* has no quality; that is rubbish. It's been sat on the shelf for years. Scratch it with your nail, it'll fall to pieces...

ELIJAH: It's not that bad...

URELE: You should see Vuvche's. Lovely.

ELIJAH: Whatever. I'll take it.

FRAIDELE: Should I... wrap it?

URELE: Hang on, hang on; let's think this through...

ELIJAH: What's to think through. I'm tired of looking for this stupid bit of rope.

FRAIDELE: The Cripple Vuvche. He stands in front of his shop all day long: no customers. Tell me; what wrong has Vuvche done you?

ELIJAH: I'm not interested in Vuvche.

URELE: *(With biting sarcasm.)* Lay'day nokelach, ungeschmoltsen, ach.

FRAIDELE: The poor always get shafted.

ELIJAH: You're wrapping it, why are you wrapping it – now you're unwrapping it: don't unwrap, just give me the rope and let –

URELE: Fine. He hates cripples: okay. However, at the end of the street, there's that mule, Mordche Peltz, a very stubborn man. Standing in the doorway of his store – no customers. You could go there. Or there's fat Volodya; big man, little shop.

ELIJAH: No, what are you – stop wrapping! Forget it. I'll just hang it around my neck.

Pulls on the rope, FRAIDELE pulls it back.

FRAIDELE: Vuvche…

ELIJAH: I don't give a –

FRAIDELE: Fat Volodya! Mordche Peltz? Would you let him starve, that mule Mordche Peltz?

ELIJAH: Don't give me all this! There's your money.

FRAIDELE: Here's your money!

ELIJAH: It's your money!

FRAIDELE: Keep your money!

Elijah lets go of the rope and FRAIDELE falls.

Music.

ELIJAH: Fraidele! This is an hour of great grace: wish for anything and it's yours. Even if you wish for… for all the money of Reb Rothschild of Frankfurt…

FRAIDELE: Oh dear…

ELIJAH: … for the diamond earrings and inlaid brooch of
Aunty Rothschild…

FRAIDELE: Oh dear, oh dear…

ELIJAH: … or the golden ships of Uncle Baruch from
Antwerp, the crown jewels. What do you desire,
Fraidele?

FRAIDELE: I… don't know. (*To URELE.*) What do we
desire?

URELE: What?

ELIJAH: What do you desire?

URELE: What do we desire?

ELIJAH: What, what? What do you desire?

FRAIDELE: We desire…

URELE: We desire… we desire that with the help of God, I
might be able to recite the prayer beginning 'Blessed is
He whose utterance created skies…' with as much
devotion as my sweet Fraidele.

ELIJAH: Amen!

AVRUMENKO takes off the Polish peasant's fur coat.

AVRUMENKO: You see how much love Urele felt for his
wife? He never left her side, even to go further than a
few paces.

MOYSHELE: And when they were together – contrary to
the rules for every man who is a true believer – he never
turned away from her…

AVRUMENKO: What, never?

MOYSHELE: ...never, ever downcast his eyes. He always looked her straight in the eye.

FRAIDELE: *(Whispers.)* Blessed is He whose utterance created skies...

URELE: *(Whispers.)* Blessed is He whose utterance created skies!

TOGETHER: *(Yelling.)* BLESSED IS HE WHOSE UTTERANCE CREATED SKIES!

FRAIDELE puts a note on the door of the shop: CLOSED.

MOYSHELE: The Great Maggid of Mezhirech said that Urele knew his wife as innocently as Adam and Eve before the fall.

AVRUMENKO: Holy Urele and holy Fraidele lived together as if in Eden.

Music: 'The Saint's Dance in Eden' (a dance using the rope).

MOYSHELE: The Holy Chochem of Koritz, Wisest of the Wise said...

AVRUMENKO: What did he say?

MOYSHELE: He said: male camels and female camels mate with their backs to each other, therefore the camel is the stupidest of all animals. With other animals the male mounts the female with his belly to her back, so these animals are a bit wiser. But humans meet face to face – and that is why humans are so wise.

THE GIRL: *(Singing.)*

– Whither is thy beloved gone,
O thou fairest among women?
– My beloved is gone down into his garden,
To the beds of spices,

To feed in the gardens,
And to gather lilies…

AVRUMENKO: The Holy Scripture connects heaven and earth. The *Song of Solomon* connects heaven and the infinite. That's why no one can completely understand it.

MOYSHELE: Except, maybe, Fraidele.

AVRUMENKO: But Urele wishes for something else. He longs for a holy person who can show him the right way to God.

THE GIRL: He doesn't stay with Fraidele.

AVRUMENKO: He puts on his gartl and starts off across the marsh, through filth and horse carcasses –

THE GIRL: – through dilapidated villages, sinking towns –

MOYSHELE: – finally crossing a rotting wooden plank for a footbridge he steps into the radiance of the shining city of–

AVRUMENKO: Lysychansk!

FRAIDELE sleeps. URELE puts on his gartl, i.e. he ties the rope around his waist three times, and leaves through the door, careful that the bell is not too loud.

Music ends.

2
(Holy Rebe Reb Elimelech)

MOYSHELE: The Emperor Joseph II was ruling in Vienna. But in Lysychansk, holy Rebe Reb Elimelech ruled, and the relations between the two rulers were sometimes tense.

The holy Menachem Mendel of Rimanov happens to be visiting Lysychansk. And when a saint visits a saint, they drink *káva* from the same cup, as if they are brothers.

MOYSHELE (as holy Reb Menachem MENDEL) sits at the end of the long table next to holy Rebe Reb ELIMELECH. They drink coffee.
MENDEL lifts up the cup, takes a sip and puts it down.
ELIMELECH lifts up the cup, takes a sip and puts it down.
MENDEL lifts up the cup, takes a sip and puts it down.
ELIMELECH lifts up the cup, takes a sip and puts it down.
MENDEL lifts up the cup, takes a sip and puts it down.

AVRUMENKO: Over a hundred Hassids sat in the room, watching with awe and devotion how exquisitely the saints took their coffee. But what those hundred Hassids couldn't see was that at the other side of the empire a petition was being put before the emperor, Joseph II…

AVRUMENKO takes off his Hassidic caftan revealing the jacket of an Austrian officer. He sits down at the other end of the table.

SECRETARY (THE GIRL.): The petition, Your Highness.

EMPEROR (AVRUMENKO.): Bloody hell? What now? What petition?

SECRETARY: The petition you requested? Requiring all young Jewish men to serve in the army?

EMPEROR: Yes, yes! Excellent. Let's get those kosher bastards to rip the innards out of the stinking chazamogen French. Yes, yes. Dismissed.

Beat.

SECRETARY: If your Highness would be so kind as to sign the –

EMPEROR: Yes. Where do I put my signature??

SECRETARY: Where it says, 'Signature of His Highness' Your Highness.

EMPEROR: Yes. My quill?

SECRETARY: Behind Your Highness' ear...

EMPEROR: Yes. My golden inkwell?

SECRETARY: On the table. Your Highness.

EMPEROR: Does it have any ink?

SECRETARY: It's full to the brim.

(Dipping his pen in the ink.) Yes, yes, yes. This is how we make laws and administer justice, my dear. You see how the world progresses: instead of the caftan we'll give the Jews uniforms. Instead of the skullcap they'll get helmets. And to replace the Talmud, a nice front loading, long barrelled –

At that moment MENDEL is lifting the cup. Suddenly ELIMELECH gives him a shove and the coffee spills over him. At exactly the same time the golden inkwell tips over and the ink spills onto the paper.

SECRETARY: Oh, bad luck, Your Highness.

EMPEROR: Bad luck? Moron! That's not bad luck, that's treason! Send me the court sorceress on the double. *(He slips in the ink.)*

At the other end of the table (ie the other end of the empire):

MENDEL: What are you doing? You'll have all of us thrown into prison?

ELIMELECH: Shhhh, shhhh why so jumpy?

MENDEL: Or do you think that your own people are cowards, that our boys would shit their pants if the emperor handed them a gun and put them in uniform.

ELIMELECH: He can dress them in uniform to his hearts content. But only if the food in the mess hall is kosher and killing on Saturdays is strictly forbidden...

MENDEL: The Talmud allows killing in *self-defence.* And the compassionate heart of this emperor means he won't go invading –

ELIMELECH: Of course! Let's drink to the emperor's compassionate heart. *(Pours coffee.)* Hedad.

MENDEL: *(Pours the coffee onto ELIMELECH.)* Here you go, you green... belly... face.

Beat.

MOYSHELE: *(Stepping out of MENDEL's role.)* Thus spoke the saints. And though the assembled Hassids listened intently they could make neither head nor tale of the sublime and mysterious words being uttered.

SORCERESS (SARAH.): *(Enters.)* Your Highness?

EMPEROR: Your crystal ball. Where is your crystal –

SORCERESS: *(Conjures it up.)* Your Highness...

EMPEROR: Well stop staring at me like you've never seen an emperor and start gazing into that thing. I want to know... I want to know who it is that keeps making things like this happen.

Crystal ball-music.
ELIMELECH covers his face with his hands.

EMPEROR: Well, what is it? What? Can you see him? Can you see him or not?

SORCERESS: I see…

EMPEROR: What?

SORCERESS: I see… hmmm.

EMPEROR: What? What do you see? Do you see his face? Who is it? Who do you see?

SORCERESS: I see two *hands…*

EMPEROR: Hands? What hands?

SORCERESS: I see two hands in the distance…

EMPEROR: Forget his hands, what about his face?

SORCERESS: His face is… concealed.

EMPEROR: Bastard! Well, has he got a beard?

SORCERESS: Beard? N-ooo… or maybe… I… can't see that, I'm afraid… All I see are –

EMPEROR: Side locks. Do you see two curly side locks?

SORCERESS: Not side-locks, but…

EMPEROR: What? What do you see, you old…?

SORCERESS: His fingers…

EMPEROR: Forget his bloody fingers!

SORCERESS: And out of each finger I see three pillars of holy fire extending into the heavens, and on each pillar of fire dance three seraphs with gleaming swords –

EMPEROR: Get out! *(Crumples up the inky petition.)* Forget it! Forget it you… civilians! Bloody kosher boys – Here's your petition! (*Throws it away.*)

Music.

MOYSHELE: And this is the story of how Jewish boys were protected from military service under the reign of Joseph II – all thanks to Reb Elimelech's holy coffee mug – may the light of his merits protect us. And it is the same holy Elimelech of Lysychansk that Urele is now journeying to, in the hope that this great and wise saint can show him the way to God…

AVRUMENKO becomes Shiye, the bocher of ELIMELECH.

ELIMELECH: Hang on… Where is the new bocher, who arrived from Lemberg?

SHIYE (AVRUMENKO.): He's disappeared! Like… he was… like smoke, he's… or maybe the earth swallowed him, and –

ELIMELECH: *(Looks under the table.)* Are you afraid, boy?

URELE: I'm afraid, holy Rebe.

ELIMELECH: What are you afraid of?

URELE: I fear… God.

ELIMELECH: And do you fear me?

URELE: I fear you.

ELIMELECH: Yes?

URELE: Yes.

ELIMELECH: How much do you fear me?

URELE: (*Thinks.*) Very, very much.

(*Thinks.*) No. Not that much.

Kind of… average.

ELIMELECH: Doesn't the Talmud say: 'you should fear
your Teacher as much as you fear the Lord.' – Where are
you off to, bocher?

URELE: I'm going to look for my Teacher, whom I fear as
much as the Lord.

ELIMELECH: Wait, let me ask you something first…

URELE: Well… okay, but could you speak quicker?

Climbs out from under the table.

ELIMELECH: Tell me, bocher…

URELE: Yes?

Pause.

ELIMELECH: Why did our Father Abraham not burn in
the fiery furnace?

URELE: In the fiery furnace?

Pause. ELIMELECH tries again.

ELIMELECH: Why did our Father Abraham not burn in
the fiery furnace?

URELE: Because God performed a miracle.

Beat.

ELIMELECH: Let's start from the beginning… King
Nimrod ordered Abraham to be thrown into-

URELE: The fiery furnace.

ELIMELECH: The fiery furnace, that's right. King Nimrod
summoned the chief minister and said to him: 'Here's a
quintal of wood, go burn Abraham to death in the fiery

furnace.' The chief minister took the wood, stashed half of it away for winter, and summoned the deputy-minister: 'Here's fifty kilos of wood, go and burn Abraham to death in the fiery furnace.' The deputy-minister also put away half of the wood and summoned the chief executioner: 'Here is twenty-five kilos of wood, go and burn Abraham to death in the fiery furnace.' The chief executioner called the deputy-executioner and said: 'Here's twelve and a half kilos of wood, go and burn Abraham to death in the fiery furnace.' Now. Who did the deputy-executioner summon?

URELE: Abraham?

ELIMELECH: His wife. He called his wife and said: 'Here are these two planks, go hide them in the shed' Now, tell me, bocher: why didn't Abraham burn in the fiery furnace?

URELE: Well, because... because... because...

ELIMELECH: You said: 'The Lord performed a miracle'...

URELE: (*Shocked.*) You mean he didn't perform a miracle?

ELIMELECH: Of course he did. Blessed be His name. But *what* was the miracle in this story?

URELE: I... I...

ELIMELECH: It was a miracle that Abraham didn't freeze to death in the fiery furnace!

Pause. Waits for laughter. None comes.

Geddit?

Beat.

URELE: Yes.

Pause.

Can I go now?

ELIMELECH: Reb Holy Chochem, the Wisest of Wise, said – 'Every thing of joy comes from Paradise – even good jokes.' I'll tell you another. Shall I tell you another?

URELE: Well... yes, okay, tell me another, holy Rebe...

ELIMELECH: From the Talmud?

URELE: Fine.

ELIMELECH: Once, the rabbis were arguing over a law. They had just reached a conclusion when this one rabbi, Eliezer, who still did not agree, stood up and called on the Lord as a witness to his truth.
Suddenly, a voice comes from on high: 'Eliezer is right.'
The rabbis were furious and they jumped up and started to shout 'Lord, Lord. Our dispute is here on earth and not in heaven, and on earth it is the council of rabbis that makes the decisions.'
So Eliezer was banished for obstruction of justice.
The day before yesterday I bumped into the Prophet Isaiah, and I asked him if he was there in heaven when this happened. Isaiah said, 'I was there.' 'And,' I said, 'And what?' he said. 'And what did God say when we outvoted him?' I said 'What did He say?' answered Isaiah, 'He laughed.'

He laughs.

You hear?

Isaiah said God laughed.

He laughs even harder.

URELE: But the Talmud says...

ELIMELECH: What does it say?

URELE: 'Your mouth should never fill with laughter until the temple is Rebuilt on Mount Zion.'

ELIMELECH laughs.

ELIMELECH: Don't you get it? That's the best joke in the whole Talmud. How is that Temple to be built? The angels build it from laughter and your tears are the mortar. Here, have some vodka. Look at this boy, Shiye… This bocher Shiye moans at me all day and all night: 'Holy Rebe, Holy Rebe Reb Rebe, how is it that I've been in the Master's school for nearly three years, my side-locks are long, my face has drained of blood, my chin has this mossy beard, my back is bent, I sleep on the floor on a heap of rotten straw, my clothes are chewed by mice – so why am I not cheerful like a real Hassid?'
Shiye, come on. Show us what you've learned. Tell us a joke.

SHIYE: About what?

ELIMELECH: What a batlan! About the saints, Shiye, about the saints. Because actually – as the Holy Chochem, Wisest of the Wise said – let the Light of his merits protect us…

URELE: What did he say?

ELIMELECH: Who?

URELE: The Wisest of the Wise.

SHIYE: He said: 'Actually.' Let the Light of his merits protect us.

URELE: Didn't he say anything else?

SHIYE: Yeah, didn't he say anything else?

ELIMELECH: Yes he did.

SHIYE: Well, what did he say?

ELIMELECH: The Holy Chochem, Wisest of the Wise said: 'Actually, we spend our entire lives in a magical dream. We only return back to our true selves if someone tells us stories of the saints.' Come on, Shiye. Wake us up.

SHIYE: Reb Simche Binem...

ELIMELECH: Who is Reb Simche Binem?

SHIYE: A wood merchant in Lemberg...

URELE: Reb Simche Binem? I know him! He's a wood merchant in Lemberg.

SHIYE: Reb Simche Binem said that the spirit of Zebulon had occupied his body, for the Scriptures say: 'Zebulon lives on a beach.' Reb Simche Binem did not live on a beach. But he had been to Gdansk. Once. Oh, and Leipzig as well.

ELIMELECH: There's no sea in Leipzig.

SHIYE: From a certain point of view.

ELIMELECH: What?

SHIYE: There is a theatre in Leipzig, holy Rebe. Reb Simche Binem once went to the theatre. But not to watch plays, nothing so mundane; Reb Simche Binem went to perform. He sang in the theatre. Not on the stage with the performers, but in the audience. He sat in the dark and sang King David's Psalms during the entire performance. He would never have been seen dead in the theatre if it hadn't been for the soul of a poor, weak girl, who had gone astray and that he wanted to...
And when later in life he heard complaints about the wickedness of young people today, about how easily they give in to the lure of the tempter, Reb Simche Binem would interrupt them and say 'Hold your tongue.' He would say, 'You don't understand the lure of the modern

world, because you have never been to the theatre. But I
have been there…' *(Sighs.)*
Of course, going to the theatre is a terrible sin…

URELE: Reb Simche? That pot-bellied wood merchant?
The man who beats his horse half to death at the market
in Lemberg like a heartless slave-driver? Tell me, how
do you know that this 'Reb' Simche has been in Gdansk
and Leipzig, and in the theatre for that matter? And
anyway, where did you get the idea that this drunken pig
is a holy man?

ELIMELECH: Son, the Talmud tells us that anyone who
pretends to be crippled or lame when they are not really,
will be punished: they really will become crippled or
lame. Therefore – looking at the example of Reb Simche
Binem – we may deduce that those who pretend to be
holy when they are not really holy – will become holy
after all. As a kind of punishment…

He laughs, again.
*Music. THE GIRL and KING DAVID – in a rococo costume
with white wigs – sing a love duet from an Italian opera
buffa.*
*A fat wood merchant stands up in the auditorium and sings
a psalm at the top of his hoarse voice. The ushers drag him out.
The duet finishes. Applause, curtsy, curtain.*

3
(Holy Reb Yeybe)

MOYSHELE: Urele stayed in Lysychansk for three years at the school of holy Rebe Reb Elimelech.

SARAH: It took him three years to learn how to laugh.

MOYSHELE: But at the end of those three years he continues on his way, for he knows now that his Teacher will be one who he fears as much as he feared God Himself.

AVRUMENKO: From Lysychansk he went to Ostroh. In Ostroh he stopped at the school of holy Reb Yeybe to learn how to eat. This he learns in one evening...

On the table is a huge bowl of mash and a spoon. HOLY YEYBE and URELE perform the cleansing of hands.

YEYBE: And believe me, when the Lord created the world every being, every object and every thing that would be rejoiced. Bread crunched with joy because it knew that when we came to eat it we would throw our praise up to God, king of all the earth, for bringing bread forth from the ground. The wine was happy that we would bless 'the creator of the vine'; the trees, the vegetables, the maize, the wheat and the barley were ecstatic to think that we would thank 'the creator of the earths bounty'. Goats, cows, rams, sheep all danced and leapt and the ducks quacked insanely, unable to contain the profound and explosive joy in their hearts, swimming races with the fish. All these wonderful animals could hardly wait for the moment when the Hassids would fry their flesh and praise god for it! Water gurgled, brandy chuckled. Even the sweet scented grasses giggled foolishly, because they knew that when we'd smell them...

He sniffs into the bowl. He pulls it in front of him and starts to eat.
URELE watches him.
Music: the gobbling song. It follows the rhythm of the eating, as YEYBE throws himself at the food gorging himself with passion at an incredible pace. Then he starts to slow, almost unnoticeably (the music following), working through the bowl of mash – then suddenly he stops – pause – he closes his eyes, prays, and then starts all over again, now chomping every morsel – finally only a single violin is creaking...
Meanwhile SARAH, AVRUMENKO and the others urge him on:

SARAH: (*As if feeding a child.*) This one's for the Father.

AVRUMENKO: This one's for Sarah.

THE GIRL: This one's for Isaac.

MOYSHELE: This one's for Jacob.

SARAH: This one's for Esau.

MOYSHELE: This one's for Joseph.

THE GIRL: This one's for Benjamin.

AVRUMENKO: This one's for Reuben.

SARAH: This one's for Pharaoh.

MOYSHELE: This one's for Moses.

AVRUMENKO: This one's for Aaron.

KING DAVID (first musician.): This one's for David.

THE GIRL: This one's for Goliath.

SARAH: This one's for Esther.

AVRUMENKO: This one's for Hamman.

YEYBE: Yuck. (*Spits it out.*)

SECOND VIOLIN PLAYER: This one's for Solomon.

BASS PLAYER: This one's for the Temple.

MOYSHELE: This one's for Zion.

SARAH: This one's for Hillel.

CLARINET PLAYER: This one's for Rabbi Akiva.

KING DAVID: This one's for Joshua ben Levi.

AVRUMENKO: This one's for Mordechai ben Rikel.

THE GIRL: This one's for the Rambam.

KING DAVID: This one's for holy Rebe Reb Yoynisn Aybeshitz.

SECOND VIOLIN PLAYER: This one's for Rabbi Loew of Prague.

CLARINET PLAYER: This one's for the Goylem.

AVRUMENKO: This one's for Baal Shem Tov.

MOYSHELE: Two for Baal-Shem-Tov.

KING DAVID: This one's for the Great Maggid.

SECOND VIOLIN PLAYER: This one's for the holy Grandfather of Spule.

MOYSHELE: This one's for Holy Chochem...

EVERYONE: ... the Wisest of the Wise!

THE GIRL: This one's for Avraham, the Angel.

BASS PLAYER: This one's for holy Rebe Reb Shmelke.

CLARINET PLAYER: This one's for holy Rebe Pinchasl.

AVRUMENKO: This one's for holy Rebe Reb Zishe.

MOYSHELE: This one's for holy Rebe Reb Elimelech.

YEYBE: No! Let him stuff his own face.

AVRUMENKO: This one's for the Seer of Lublin.

KING DAVID: This one's for Shloymele of Karlyn.

BASS PLAYER: This one's for Aaron of Belz.

CLARINET PLAYER: This one's for Yitzhak Eyzik Toub of Nagykálló.

YEYBE: This one's for Yeybe.

THE GIRL: This one's for Gog.

SARAH: This one's for Magog.

BASS PLAYER: This one's for Tehom.

CLARINET PLAYER: This one's for Behom.

URELE: This one's for Reb Simche Binem.

But this morsel won't go down.

URELE: This one's for Reb Simche Binem.

ALL: Reb Simche Binem. Reb Simche Binem.

Silence.
YEYBE stops, the music halts…

YEYBE: And you, the rest of you… you souls, still exiled to the nice and fatty barbulyes blessed with scented buckwheat, you souls who long for eternal light, forgive me! But Yeybe can eat no more. (*Talking to the food.*) Maybe next time…

YEYBE collapses under the table.
URELE pulls the bowl over and finishes off the leftovers.

4
(The Virgin)

Music: whispers of the forest...

SARAH: It's dark. But Urele feels no fear in the forest. He fears only God almightily, and –

MOYSHELE: – the unknown, the one who would make his knees tremble and tongue-tied – his Teacher. The one he searched for.

AVRUMENKO: The forest whispers. Urele stumbling over roots, slips on wet branches, the trees stretching out into the darkness in all directions –

SARAH: But Urele was not afraid. No. But...

You do feel a bit... odd when you realise that you're wandering alone through the endless deep, dark forest, all alone, at night, in silence except for that sound, that sound that sounds like the hot breath of an animal following behind –

MOYSHELE: Urele spots a glimmer of light in the distance.

AVRUMENKO: The closer he gets, the brighter it shines. A few more steps...

SARAH: Branches parted...

MOYSHELE: And...

Beat.

SARAH: Never had he seen such... beauty!

GIRL: Where've you come from?

URELE: Ostroh.

GIRL: Where are you going?

URELE: Koritz.

GIRL: And who have you to account to?

URELE: Well... At the school of holy Rebe Reb Elimelech I learned how to laugh. Then in Ostroh, at the school of holy Reb Yeybe I learned a great and sublime secret: I learned how to eat. But I still haven't found my Teacher...

GIRL: Holy Yeybe is a wise man. Once, someone was complaining about a Hassid, saying that he was a glutton, that he'd eaten a whole goose...

URELE: A goose?

GIRL: In one sitting.

URELE: Not a duck?

GIRL: No.

URELE: In one sitting?

GIRL: And Yeybe said: 'Leave him be; it's his only passion...'

URELE: Blessed is he who knows only one passion.

GIRL: Hmnn. But a good man should not be a glutton.

URELE: True. He should avoid eating an entire goose. If at all possible.

GIRL: Urele?

URELE: Yes?

GIRL: Come closer.

URELE: (*Beat.*) Yes.

GIRL: Do you know who I am?

URELE: I… well, when I saw you I felt this, my… my knees trembled and my, my, my tongue sort of, it beca… became tied… and… and… and… You are my Teacher! Are you my Teacher?

GIRL: 'The one for whom only knowledge is important and nothing else is like the ungodly.'

URELE: Those are the words of the Talmud!

GIRL: Bring that hairy face over here. I've got something I want to teach you. First, tell me the theory of the gartl. *(Starts to untie the gartl on URELE's waist.)*

URELE: The… the theory of the gartl. Yes. Alright. Its two ends are decorated with… tassels. The gartl has to be long enough to go around one's waist three times… and… and…

GIRL: And… *(Starts to unwind it.)*

URELE: The gartl is worn all day long, especially during prayer, furthermore during the study of the Scriptures, during meals, and always. The Talmud tells us: the Lord made only the *upper* part of man's body in His own image, therefore, the gartl is the boundary between man's human half and animal half, preventing the heart from seeing shame…

GIRL: And what does God's *lower* half look like?

She pulls off the gartl. URELE tries to grab it but fails.

URELE: When we put our gartl on in the morning, we say a blessing, we say 'Blessed are You, O Lord our God, King of the Universe –'

GIRL: And make sure the gartl never has a knot on it. *(Tickles him.)* Because the devil slides around your waist during prayer looking for something to grab onto, and if he finds a knot, he will use it to cling on and devour

45

your prayer as it comes out of your mouth, why don't you look at me?

URELE: A holy man never looks at women. A holy man, if he happens to find himself speaking to a woman, looks out of a window.

GIRL: Can't see any windows, Urele.

URELE: Windows are the symbols of secrets.

GIRL: Look at me!

URELE: A holy man doesn't even look at his wife! Ever! At his slightly plump, but very attractive, actually, wife who –

GIRL: Liar.

URELE: There is a story in the Talmud about a man who only discovered that his wife had a wooden leg at her funeral. That man was a saint.

GIRL: What is my leg made of?

URELE: What?

GIRL: They say it's made of porcelain. What do you think?

URELE: Well, it's white. But I don't think it's made of porcelain.

GIRL: What makes you say that?

URELE: There's no crack in it and it is not chipped. And... and the Talmud says that, that a porcelain leg is a fragile more than is a fragile, is much more fragile than flesh, than sin, than a feather...

GIRL: Why don't you touch it and make sure?

URELE starts to tie his phylacteries on.

URELE: The gartl should be tied around the body three times, but the phylacteries, the prayer straps, should be tied *seven* times! We Hassids twist it on away from our bodies, while the Talmudists twist it towards themselves. This is because they are selfish and think only of themselves, where as we think of all humanity. But the phylacteries can only be owned by those who are pure in body and soul. For in each black square there is the most radiant name of the Lord written, and if our prayer strap is on we must keep it in mind continuously. This is not easy. This is not easy. It speaks of retribution and punishment, and anyone who does not keep this in mind puts on his prayer strap in vain.

GIRL: You're grinding your teeth.

URELE: 'As if he would have fastened stones on his head and arm.'

GIRL: I've seen you before, walking through the forest, many times. Always alone. Like me. I often asked myself, when will he come to me? But you're always in your own world when you're walking. What's the matter? I'm pure –

URELE: What? Satan is a virgin!

GIRL: We'll see.

URELE: Your hair sweeps the ground, it's not cut like Jewish women's.

GIRL: Come on. I bathed in the stream, I've made a soft bed, prepared a rich feast... At least look at me, Urele.

URELE: I don't need to. I know that your hair ripples like blades of grass caressed by the wind, that the tips of your breasts glow like strawberries...

GIRL: (*Caressing him.*) My little bunny...

URELE: (*Trying to resist, but not making a very good job of it.*)
At every moment, especially moments when we think we
will not be able to control ourselves we must imagine a
great, a terrible fire, a terrible fire burning in front of us,
and we throw ourselves into that fire, for the glory of
God! Our minds must never be idle. And every time we
feel the sensation of pleasure we must use our minds and
imagine how much greater the pleasure would be,
immeasurably greater if someone came and dragged us
from our food, if someone tore us from our love making
and we died the most painful death imaginable. But you
have to be careful with this kind of thinking, because if
you dwell on these things too much, you might find
yourself becoming attracted to gluttonousness or you
might find yourself jumping on the first woman who...

She is kissing his neck.

GIRL: Shhhhhh...

URELE: And in order to recover we must concentrate our
thoughts on the section of the Talmud that says: 'Where
have you come from?' 'A putrid drop.' 'Where are you
going?' 'To decay.' 'And who do you have to account to?'

GIRL: To me...

URELE: Nooooo! NO!

Darkness.

SARAH: 'In the beginning I fasted a great deal,' said the
Seraph, holy Reb Urele, late in life. 'In the beginning I
fasted a great deal because I wanted to teach my body to
live with the light of my soul. But once, in a clearing in
a forest, I had such a miraculous experience, that my
soul learned how to live with the darkness of my body.'

Music.

5
(Holy Chochem)

HOLY CHOCHEM: We must live in ignorance. We must tend the ignorance of our souls as we would the fowl in our gardens.

AVRUMENKO: So said Holy Chochem of Koritz, the Wisest of Wise.

HOLY CHOCHEM: Modesty and humility.

MOYSHELE: So humble is the Holy Chochem that he speaks to his dog with as much respect as if he were addressing his Teacher.

SARAH: There was a man living with him at his house who helped out with the animals, Yude Hersh. This Yude Hersh is over forty years old, completely illiterate and doesn't even have a wife – he was an um-mentsh, a very crude type of man.

HOLY CHOCHEM: Whenever I see that Yude Hersh, I always tremble with respect. What a holy man. If he brings someone food, even a goose, even if he brings oats to a goose he almost melts with humility.

Yude Hersh? Is it true that you are as humble as our Father Moses, who was the most humble man since the creation of the world.

YUDE HERSH: Oh yeah, easy. I'm as humble as him. I, Yude Hersh, a simple um-mentsh am as humble and meek as holy Rebe Reb Moyshele. Can I ask something?

HOLY CHOCHEM: I'm listening, Yude Hersh.

YUDE HERSH: The Hassids say that if we tell a story about the great Baal Shem Tov the night after Sabbath, then it has a good effect on the whole weeks trade. Is this true?

HOLY CHOCHEM: Yes, my son, it's true.

YUDE HERSH: Great. I've got a sack of oats I want to shift.

HOLY CHOCHEM: Gitz gepoylt. May you be lucky in –

YUDE HERSH: Amen.

HOLY CHOCHEM: But it is not only good for trade, and not only on Saturday night, and not only does it apply to stories about the Great Baal Shem Tov, but about any saint and–

YUDE HERSH: About me, for example?

HOLY CHOCHEM: For example, about you.

YUDE HERSH: Right, let's see; there was this sickly bocher –

HOLY CHOCHEM: What bocher?

YUDE HERSH: You remember? At Purim? Looked like a sack of bones. Even you prayed for him, and still he dropped dead –

HOLY CHOCHEM: Ah, no, I think you've got that wrong, Yude Hersh, it was –

YUDE HERSH: Right, so there was this sickly bocher, and he lay there with the angel of death at his head, the Malakhha-mavet, with his sword dripping three drops of poison into the bocher's mouth –

HOLY CHOCHEM: Three? Were you counting?

YUDE HERSH: I wasn't just counting.

HOLY CHOCHEM: What else were you doing?

YUDE HERSH: Don't you remember?

HOLY CHOCHEM: I seem to have forgotten.

YUDE HERSH: Well, I flew up to heaven, right, and I saw that the gate of life had been slammed shut, right in his face. I knocked. I cried. I begged and thumped on the door – but in vain. So I went over to the Provisions Bureau and the door was wide open, walked in and asked for as much food for this bocher as I could carry.

HOLY CHOCHEM: Did they give him food?

YUDE HERSH: Twenty… one-hundred and twenty sacks. What happened was the Provisions Bureau asked the Life Bureau if the man's fate was sealed and they said yes. So the Provisions Bureau official thought to himself: 'Why not give poor soul food, he's not going to eat it anyway.' So, I picked up the sacks…

HOLY CHOCHEM: All one hundred and twenty sacks?

YUDE HERSH: One hundred and twenty sacks, yeah, and I took them over to the Life Bureau. As soon as they saw me coming they closed the gate. So I started yelling: 'Give him life!' I shouted 'We won't!' they shouted. So I started waving these sacks around –

HOLY CHOCHEM: One hundred and twenty sacks?

YUDE HERSH: – and I said, 'I see that the Life Bureau wishes to twist the truth of the Talmud. Or doesn't the Talmud say, 'To whom does God give food?', 'Only those whom he gives life' – And since the Provisions Bureau gave this man such a large amount of food –

HOLY CHOCHEM: One hundred and twenty sacks.

YUDE HERSH: – then you are required to give him a life to match, otherwise you un-be-rufen the truth of the Talmud.'

What could they do?

HOLY CHOCHEM: What?

YUDE HERSH: Nothing. They opened the gate – and the bocher rose from his sickbed, and walks around to this day as healthy as a gentile. Don't you remember?

HOLY CHOCHEM: Yude Hersh, have you read it?

YUDE HERSH: What?

HOLY CHOCHEM: The Talmud.

Beat.

YUDE HERSH: No.

Beat.

They haven't either.

HOLY CHOCHEM: Where are you going?

YUDE HERSH: Told the story. I'm taking these oats to market.

HOLY CHOCHEM: Gitz gepoylt. Have you watered the geese?

YUDE HERSH: Probably not. I can hear them squawking like lame… angels.

Exits.

HOLY CHOCHEM: 'Yude Hersh'. Truly, what an incredible saint. It is the great tragedy of my life that I can never hope to be as perfect as he is.

Music.

MOYSHELE: Our heavenly Torah has 600,000 letters. There are 600,000 souls scattered among our people.

Each soul is equal to a letter of the Torah. And if a single letter is missing the Torah becomes invalid.

SARAH: In the same way as the letters come together to form words and the words come together to form sentences, so the souls must come together. But why is it forbidden for the letters to join?

Pause.

Because each soul has to have a few hours to be *alone* with their Creator.

AVRUMENKO: Urele comes out of the forest blinking into a brilliant summer's day. Straight away he heads for Koritz, longing with his entire heart that he might at last find his Teacher. Because in Koritz, the holy Chochem, Wisest of Wise is ruling.

SARAH: By the time he gets there the leaves have fallen. In the town square, Ukrainian peasants tend their horses, Jews in caftans run to and fro, their side-locks sailing in the wind, and an um-mentsh is herding his geese, barking orders at them like a sergeant major.

MOYSHELE: And in the gateway of the Prayer House stands an old man, his hair white…

HOLY CHOCHEM: Bore habe.

URELE: Bore nimtse.

Pause.

HOLY CHOCHEM: Depart in peace, I am not your Teacher.

Enters into the Prayer House.

URELE: Bore tiheye.

YUDE HERSH: Oh well, never mind. Don't be sad, bocher – there is a lesson to be found in this; there's cholent, fragrant, juicy, made of the very best goose, but if you eat it you'll vomit. There's vintage wine, but no matter how much of it you drink someone else will get drunk. This is the truth of the Talmud and –

URELE is gone.

Hey, wait! Where are you going? Oi!

Hurries after URELE.

6.
(Aaron, the Messiah)

AVRUMENKO: There is a messiah in every generation. He lives a solitary existence, unable to reveal himself to us because of our sin. But once, the whole world knew that the messiah lived here, in Belz, and his name was –

MADAME bursts on past AVRUMENKO, brushing him aside. She is formidable, rich, and beautiful, and she demands music from the band to accompany her entrance. Satisfied, she shuts them up and heads for AARON.

MADAME (SARAH.): Please: don't bother to kiss my hand.

AARON: Don't worry, Madame; we're not French…

MADAME: Worry? Don't be ridiculous. I never worry. One should never worry. There is only one thing one should worry about and that's that one worries

AARON: But Madame, this *bon mot* is not your own. It was first said by Reb Motyele of Lechowitz –

MADAME: Are you the messiah?

AARON nods.

Stop nodding, little knight, and say straight out: 'Yes, Madame, I, Aaron of Belz, am the messiah.'

AARON: How's your Hebrew, Madame?

MADAME: Better than yours, I should imagine.

AARON: Then perhaps you know what the word *ayin* means. It means –

MADAME: Nothing.

AARON: And the word *aniy,* which means –

MADAME: Me. It means me.

AARON: The same set of letters, but in a different order. The world of God is one word and our little selves are not separate but merge together to make that word...

MADAME: What are you suggesting? That *I* merge with you?

AARON: ...and so, if you want to know if Mr X is the messiah, then simply ask him, 'Are you the messiah?' And if he answers, 'Yes, *I* am,' then you can be sure that Mr X is only a very simple, insignificant, loud mouth, have a seat please.

The Madame does not sit down. She looks around.

Because who dares to call themselves *Me,* when only the Lord has the right to do that?

MADAME: So. This is where *He* lives. In this hovel. How is it possible for you, Mr X, to pray every day and say the words, 'Blessed is He who provides me with all I need' – for you have been provided with nothing.

AARON: Which is exactly what I need, so –

MADAME: Whatever, as the holy Rebe Reb Yoynisn Aybeshitz says – (*Pointing to a point on the wall.*) What on earth is this?

AARON: *Excusé*, Madame, but when they were building that part of the wall, I wasn't present. Neither were my prayers. That little part there was made only of bricks and mortar.

Madame punches the bricks out. The wind howls through.

Tea?

MADAME: *Merci.*

AARON: Lechaim.

They sit and have tea.

AARON: You live in Paris?

MADAME: Please! I live in Switzerland, in my palace at
    Coppet. Tell me, have you ever been to Geneva?

AARON: Hmm. Is it a nice city?

MADAME: It is a shithole.

AARON: And Belz? How do you like Belz?

MADAME: Haven't you got any sugar?

AARON: Of course. It's there on the shelf. Can you see it
    from here or shall I move it a bit closer?

MADAME: You want me to *stare* at your sugar?

AARON: Why, what do you do with it in your palace in
    Coppet?

MADAME: Put it in the tea?

AARON: But then it dissolves!

MADAME: *Tant pis!* The cupboard is full.

AARON: (S*ighs.*) And thus bit by bit, the entire cupboard
    ends up in the tea…

MADAME: Tell me, do you think I'm an idiot?

AARON: Scripture says: 'there's no agreement in my bones
    because of my sins', yes? – Why is it that the eye can
    only see, the ear can only hear, the tongue can only
    taste? Why? Because of the sin of Eve. Correct?

MADAME: *Tant pis.*

AARON: But whoever purifies themselves to the *roots of
    their soul* is able to see with their *ear* and feel with their
    tongue –

MADAME: And hear with their nose, and smell with their ear, and look with their tongue, and look with their ears, and even look with their nose, and feel and taste with their eyes –

AARON: Correct! That person can taste sweets with their eyes, for example, that sugar on the shelf…

MADAME: May I taste it?

AARON: Be my guest.

She sticks her finger in AARON's tea.

MADAME: Mmmmm. Delicious.

AARON: Blessed is he who created tea leaves.

MADAME: Amen. I'm here to present you with a very great secret; that which you need to keep in mind whenever you pronounce the greatest principle of our faith 'Hear O, Israel. The Lord is our God. The Lord is One.' For this you will bless my name every single day.

AARON: Amen. Let's hear the secret.

MADAME: I don't want the Jews to hear *(Looks around.).*

AARON: Holy Ari says: 'A secret is that which is pronounced for all to hear, and still no one hears it.'

MADAME: Yes, well this secret cannot be found in the writings of holy Ari. Nor in the writings of Rambam. This secret was made known to me from above… *(She whispers in his ear.)* See? 'Hear O, Israel. The Lord is our God. The Lord is One.' See?

She whispers in his ear again as if she might nibble it.

AARON: I see.

MADAME: And what about you? Anything to add?

AARON: Nothing.

MADAME: 'Nothing'? So you just bleat like a sheep?

AARON: Exactly. Just close my eyes and cry: Hear O
Israel, THE LORDISOURGODTHELORDISONE...'

All the cups fall, another wall collapses.

AARON: You try it.

MADAME: You Poles... Is it not written: *(Sarcastic.)* 'Walk
humbly with the Lord your God.'

AARON: Yes but to be humble, Madame, you have to be
very clever.

MADAME: Wow.

AARON: You're staring?

MADAME: I'm looking at this mountain. This little pile of
earth really had to boast quite a lot for it to become
so huge.

He laughs.

Master! Tell me, Master, how can one reach the truth?

AARON: Truth cannot be reached, my dear lady. God looks
upon those who devote their entire life to truth and gives
them a little piece of it, for free. A tiny pinch. Like this
pinch of tobacco. Or maybe less, it is only truth.

MADAME: *(Pinches a bit of tobacco.)* Is this much enough for
a Messiah?

AARON: Whatever, as holy Rebe Reb Yoynisn Aybeshitz
says.

MADAME: Mind if I pinch a bit of your truth?

She fills her pipe.

Do you have a light?

AARON: With the greatest of pleasure. My children, some fire for the lady.

There is a loud hiss.

AARON: What's the matter?

AVRUMENKO: The fire's gone out.

AARON: Okay. Then bring an ember.

Another hiss.

AVRUMENKO: The embers have turned to icicles.

AARON: Okay. Then bring an icicle.

Madame...

MADAME: *(He lights her pipe with the icicle.)* Of course it is not very hard to work miracles. Everything on this earth is already a miracle.

AARON: True. Now being a Jew – that's hard.

MADAME: And being a Messiah?

AARON: If I were to be born again, I would like to be born a cow.

MADAME: A cow?

AARON: Every morning a young Jew would come and milk me and this would refresh him before he begins his daily service to God...

MADAME: Oh là là! How beautiful and brilliant this world truly is. And then man comes along, yanking at things with his little hands – the teats of a cow, for example.

AARON: And Madame? If you were to be born again? What would you like to be?

Pause. She glares at him.

Is it a secret?

MADAME: A big secret. A big, big secret. A very big, big secret. But I'll tell you. Send this lot out.

AARON: You can whisper it in my ear –

MADAME: That is not enough. All of these bochers, out.

AARON: You want me to send them out?

MADAME: Chuck 'em out.

AARON: Or else?

MADAME: Or else I won't tell you the secret.

AARON: And if you don't tell me the secret?

Pause.

AVRUMENKO: Holy Rebe –

AARON: Outside, Avrumenko. Just for a minute.

MADAME: (*To the audience.*) Now, all of you, listen to me. Can you hear me? Good. Get up, go out. Please. Leave us in private. Interval. In – ter – val. Oi, you at the back; out. And stay outside until we tell you.

The band starts playing a finale.

MADAME: (*Shouting at the band.*) And you!

The band begin to go, sulkily.

And shut the door behind you!

Interval.

PART TWO

The music of the spheres. The stars are shining in AARON's room, AARON dancing a mysterious dance with the full Moon (a phosphorescent balloon). Banging on the door.

AARON: Who's there?

FROM OUTSIDE: Me!

AARON: Who?

Pause. The wind is howling outside.

Who dares to call himself *Me,* when only the Lord has the right to –

He stops abruptly, following his own logic and is suddenly frightened of who might be on the other side of the door. He grabs the stars and squeezes them into the candleholder.

FROM OUTSIDE: Open the door, Aaron!

AARON runs around looking for somewhere to hide the moon, but the door is kicked open bursting it.

YUDE HERSH: *(Carrying URELE on his shoulder, who is covered with snow and ice.)* While you're dawdling, Aaron…

AARON: Yude Hersh?

YUDE HERSH: Who did you expect? What are you gawping at, it's just a frozen bocher. *(Putting URELE down.)* Get the fire going. Any vodka?

AARON brings the vodka.

Open wide, bocher: we'll warm you from the inside out.

He pours vodka into URELE. AARON runs out and comes back with an icicle, which he uses to start the fire.

URELE: Wh… Whe.. rarwee…

AARON: Belz.

YUDE HERSH: What?

AARON: He's asked where we are.

YUDE HERSH: *We're – in – Belz.* The ancient nest! Did
you know, bocher, that once the messiah lived here?

URELE: Whi… mess…

YUDE HERSH: And the whole world knew that the
messiah lived here, in Belz, and his name was – the same
as this nebechel's here –

AARON: Shall I make some tea?

YUDE HERSH: Don't ask – just make. The whole world
knew and was happy. Except Satan. Satan was not happy.
He couldn't get used to the idea that he had to give up
his reign now that the time had come to pass the sceptre
– so Satan krenked himself until he turned into a woman.
A fantastically beautiful woman, yes, but also – and
here's the clever part – an incredibly intelligent woman.
She travelled all over the world learning how to do
chochmeh, learning how to debate, and finally arrived at
Belz –

AARON: Sugar?

YUDE HERSH: Please.

URELE: I don't want any.

AARON: He doesn't want any? Why doesn't he want any?

URELE: She came to Belz…

YUDE HERSH: Who?

URELE: Satan!

YUDE HERSH: Oy! What a contest that was: the debate between Satan and the Messiah! It's a wonder they didn't incinerate each other with the fire of their arguments. Finally, the messiah asked a question…

URELE: What?

YUDE HERSH: No one knows. It's a very big, big secret.

AARON: He asked the woman what she would like to become.

URELE: What?

AARON: In another life. The messiah said that he would like to be a cow –

YUDE HERSH: Please! Why don't you make yourself useful and bring us some tobacco? So the messiah asked something, a secret, the Big Secret. And the woman said that she would tell him, but that the secret was so profound that everyone else had to leave the room. And when the very last person left the room, and the door was closed, then –

AARON: There's no tobacco.

YUDE HERSH: What kind of a house is this? Eh? Hasn't the Lord God, King of all creation said, 'Tobacco. Believe me, the world won't do with anything else as many good deeds as with thee! For example,' he said, 'Let's say a guest pops round for a chat and we have nothing to offer them on the way of refreshments, not a single crust of bread, or tea, or vodka, not a single drop. But if we pull out the tobacco our guest can fill their pipe, and is content – and at no great cost either. We have earned an eternal distinction through performing an act of generosity, through tobacco. Thee. ' Tobacco has no reason to complain.

AARON: I have some bread.

YUDE HERSH: Bring it out!

URELE: And what did the lady say?

YUDE HERSH: What lady?

URELE: When everyone left. And the messiah was left alone with the lady, with Satan...

AARON: She said –

YUDE HERSH: Dunno. No one knows that. And anyway, it's not important, because when the last person had left the room and the door was closed, the messiah realised, at that very moment the messiah realised –
Do you have anything to go with the bread? –

URELE: He realized that...

YUDE HERSH: That...

AARON: I've got some salt.

YUDE HERSH: Bring it out! – He realized that in the thrill of the chase he had forgotten the words of the Talmud: you are *never ever,* even for a single moment to be alone, in private with a strange woman.

He remembered these words but just a second too late. He was there with that woman. In private. His holy mission to bring about the messianic age was tainted.

AARON: All this happened on the sixth day of the month of *Tishri.* Satan was victorious.

URELE: What happened to the messiah?

YUDE HERSH: What messiah? He wasn't a messiah anymore, just a nebechel.

AARON: In England they've made a cart that runs without a horse?

Beat.

YUDE HERSH: And what does the horse do in the meantime? Run after the cart? Stupid English.

AARON: I am afraid, very afraid, that redemption will come of its own accord, through the inventions of man...

URELE: I share your fears... holy Rebe...

YUDE HERSH: 'Holy Rebe'? What are you on abou –?

AARON: Shhhh.

YUDE HERSH starts to snore immediately.

AARON: Good. Now we can debate these issues together, bocher. You bring the scrolls of theTalmud, and I'll bring this... So that we don't scorch our side-locks in the heat of the debate.

URELE: What's that?

AARON: The debating machine of the great Reb Benjamin Franklin of New York: a lightning-rod. Gitz gepoylt!

Darkness.

Lightning-music.

SARAH: They say the saints only seem to live among us here on Earth. In reality, they resemble the stars.

AVRUMENKO: 'There is a storm,' they said that night. 'A lightning storm.' The dogs hid under the bed whining, because the dogs knew that in reality, holy Reb Urele was in heaven... and holy Reb Urele was learning the art of doing chochmeh.

MOYSHELE: Reb Aaron, the fallen messiah leads the debate. And holy Reb Urele grinds the counter-arguments of the Lord, the Almighty, to dust with his wisdom, insight and humour.

AARON and URELE sit at the table, drinking heavily. They are already quite drunk and have spilt some vodka over the table.

URELE: 'Okayokayokay,' says God, 'okay, I know: a cart that runs without a horse. That's old news,' says the Lord. 'Or do you think that we don't read the London Herald Tribune up here in heaven?'

'Nevertheless, Lord,' I say, 'there's one Yude Hersh, who has not read the London Tribune Herald, has not even read the Talmud, and – may the Lord have mercy – probably doesn't even know how to read. But this meshuge, this Yude Hersh made an observation so wise that words fail it. Yude Hersh said, listen Lord, he said, 'And what does the horse do in the meantime? Run after the cart?' These were the words of Yude Hersh. He also said, 'Stupid English.''

AARON: 'That is not so', retorts the Almighty, 'that is not so. One can learn something from everybody'.

URELE: Even from the English?

AARON: Even from the English. Everyone and everything can teach us something, not only the things that *I* (meaning the Almighty) have created, but also that which man… man has made.

URELE: Man?

AARON: Man.

URELE: Okay. What does the railroad teach us?

AARON: The Lord says, 'Have you ever missed a train? And you ran after it, cursing and yanking your luggage across the ground, furious, instead of stopping, lighting your pipe and pondering the beautiful truth that the railroad revealed to us… that… that… we can miss out on everything because of one moment.

URELE: Good! And what does the…the telegraph teach us?

AARON: That every word is taken into account and charged.

URELE: Excellent! And what does the…the telephone teach us?

AARON: What's a telephone?

URELE: You say *Bore habe* in Belz, and the great Reb Benjamin answers *Bore nimtse* in New York.

AARON: Has this been invented?

URELE: Not yet. But what does it teach us?

AARON: What does it teach us?

URELE: That up there in heaven, they hear what down here on earth… I mean, that up here in heaven, we can hear what people down there on earth…

AARON: Whatever. Of course they hear everything in heaven. It's heaven. You don't have to invent a…thing… that –

URELE: And what does the cart that runs without a horse teach us?

AARON: Right. Well, that's just it… I am afraid, very afraid, that redemption will come of its own accord, through the inventions of man…

URELE: 'You speck of dust, what does it matter to you how it comes?'

AARON: It matters, my Creator, Lord Father. It matters a lot. Because if the redemption comes in the form of a miracle, if the ocean parts –

URELE: Or the sky opens –

AARON: Or something like this, then there can never be another doubtful and faithless person on this planet. But I ask, *I* ask (please excuse me Lord), that if the redemption will come in an even seemingly natural way through the inventions of man, through the telephone and whatever, the airplane, or through clicking and whirring and flashing… things, then where is the proof for those who doubt that this world is not a kind of cart that runs without a horse? Let's hear, Lord: what does the *Horse* have to say to that?

URELE: That's right. What does the Horse have to say for himself?

A huge crash.
The lightning-rod glows red-hot.

YUDE HERSH: *(Wakes up.)* What are you two up to? Babbling all night, drinking all the vodka; a whole bottle?

They are laughing and banging the table.
Darkness.

SARAH: And since then, since that night we no longer need be afraid that the redemption of humanity will be come about of it's own accord, through the inventions of man.

MOYSHELE: This is what Reb Aaron and Reb Urele have chochmehed for us.

AVRUMENKO: May the Light of their merits protect us.

MOYSHELE: Amen.

THE GIRL: Nevertheless, Urele had still not found his
Teacher – even up there in heaven.

*KING DAVID is singing a very sad song about the Messiah,
everybody humming the refrain, while MOYSHELE gets
dressed up to become the Great Maggid, the oldest Teacher,
with white side-locks.*

7
(Zishe the Fool of God)

*The GREAT MAGGID and the disciples: the young ELIMELECH,
YEYBE, HOLY CHOCHEM, Wisest of the Wise, ZISHE and
bochers.*

GREAT MAGGID: The material world is an ocean and we
tiny drops of stagnant water stagger through as
sluggishly as the catfish through the slime of the deeps.
But the prayers of passion… perhaps you too have
experienced such moments… the prayers of passion
elevate us above the material and even spiritual worlds.
They carry us up to that original point in which
everything is present; every world, every time and age,
God's great plan, everything, every thing, just like the
tree in the seed, everything in one indivisible singularity.
And this primeval, all encompassing point is the first
word of the Holy Scripture; BERESHIT. *In the
beginning.* From this little word came forth all of
existence, every creature, just as the snail comes forth
from its shell, and it is to this point that we always fly
back to when our souls are pure and empty.

Please don't think that I am delivering my sermon about
catfish and snails and all these unclean creatures just to
enrage you. But believe me, just as God created us in his
image, so he created these unclean creeping things in the
image of something. In the image of mysterious worlds.
Each little animal, in it's own way, is created in an image
of some ancient world, and these worlds existed in
infinite numbers before the creation of our own. But
don't ask me to tell you about them; these are great,
great, great, great secrets.

And now, brethren, take out the passage that I
distributed amongst you. It says 'And God said-'

ZISHE: And God said!

GREAT MAGGID: Yes. 'And God said–'

ZISHE: And God said!

GREAT MAGGID: Zishe, please.

ZISHE: Yes, holy Rebe.

GREAT MAGGID: Thank you. 'And God said–'

ZISHE: And God said!

YEYBE: Zishe!

ELIMELECH: Shut up!

HOLY CHOCHEM: Please continue, holy Rebe.

GREAT MAGGID: 'And God said–'

ZISHE: And God said! And God said!

ALL: Zishe!

ZISHE: The Lord has spoken! The word of God. *(He is in a religious ecstasy.)* And God said! And God said! And thus the Lord has spoken!

The bochers hold him down and drag him out.
Pause.
They return.

GREAT MAGGID: And God –

Beat.

Where is Zishe?

ELIMELECH: We locked him up, holy Rebe.

GREAT MAGGID: In the wood shed?

YEYBE: In the wood shed, holy Rebe.

GREAT MAGGID: Great. Hmm. Right.
'And God said–'

We can hear ZISHE pounding on the door of the wood shed.

GREAT MAGGID: 'And God –

Pause. He closes the book.

But actually… this is what I'm saying to you. Actually,
and this is exactly what I'm saying to you: if someone
truly speaks, and someone else *truly* listens, then one
word is enough, one single word is enough to purify the
world of its sins. For instance, if somebody says…

ELIMELECH: 'And God said'?

YEYBE: Or 'BERESHIT! BERESHIT!'?

HOLY CHOCHEM: Or if all he says is… is… is 'actually'?

GREAT MAGGID: Well done. Off you go.

Darkness.
Music.

SARAH: The great Baal Shem Tov wanted to save the life
of a boy who was dying, so he moulded a candle laced
with heavenly herbs, took it out to the forest and
fastened it onto a tree. The candle burned all night long,
and by morning the boy was cured.

MOYSHELE: Thirty years later the Great Maggid, disciple
of the great Baal Shem, wished to save a child from
death, but he was unfamiliar with the mystical properties
of the heavenly herbs. So he went to the shop, bought a
candle, took it out to the forest, fastened it onto a tree,
and called upon the name of his Master. By morning the
child was cured.

SARAH: Yesterday, when one of the disciples of the Great
Maggid wanted to save a child, he did not have any

money for a candle, nor did not go out into the woods either. 'We have no power,' he said. 'We no more have the power to do what our ancestors did. But I will tell you their story.' And he told of the candle, the heavenly herbs, the great Baal Shem Tov, the forest, the night. And this morning the child is healed.

AVRUMENKO: The First Gate was opened by the Great Baal Shem Tov.

MOYSHELE: Through the Second Gate came the Great Maggid.

AVRUMENKO: The Generation of Saints teemed through the Third Gate.

MOYSHELE: And the Fourth Gate?

Pause.

SARAH: Still closed. But Urele has his eye to the keyhole, and can see the Generation of Saints, can see it and is amazed. Each saint held knowledge, even these ones he'd met: one could tell a story, another could laugh, the third could eat, the fifth knew the art of chochmeh –

THE GIRL: But what did Zishe, the fool of the Lord know?

AVRUMENKO: Zishe knows how to suffer. He suffers as sweetly as a nightingale. He begs suffering door to door, and everywhere he goes they beat him up, slap him around, spit in his face, and when everyone, Hassids and non-Hassids, Polish and non-Polish, Russians and non-Russians, Hungarians and non-Hungarians, when everyone has beaten him up, slapped him around, spat in his face, then Zishe lies down on an anthill, near Hanipol, by the side of the road.

But the ants do not so much as touch his skin. Not a single little ant bites him. – 'Lord of all the World.' –

complains Zishe. – 'Am I so worthless? Not even the ants want me.'

MOYSHELE: Each holy person had a kingdom. One of them ruled in Lysychansk…

SARAH: Another ruled in Ostroh…

THE GIRL: A third ruled in Koritz…

MOYSHELE: But Zishe was the greatest of them all because he ruled over an anthill, and his tiny Hassids would swarm around him, just as when the emperor looks out of his window in the Burg, or rides his carriage down the Kärtner Strasse in Vienna.

ZISHE, URELE and YUDE HERSH are sitting on the anthill.

URELE: Holy Rebe…

YUDE HERSH: Holy Rebe…

URELE: Explain, holy Rebe –

YUDE HERSH: Please, explain to him –

URELE: Quiet, Yude Hersh.

YUDE HERSH: I'm quiet! I am quiet.

URELE: Explain the commandment in the Talmud that says –

YUDE HERSH: Hang on; which commandment?

Beat.

URELE: The commandment in the Talmud that says we are obligated to praise the Lord for the bad as-

YUDE HERSH: For the good.

URELE: No. For the bad.

YUDE HERSH: Praise him – for the bad?

URELE: Praise him for the bad. That's the point.

YUDE HERSH: It is. It's the point.

URELE: How can we praise the Lord equally for the good and bad that happens to us? Explain it to me, holy Rebe.

ZISHE: Explain it to him, Yude Hersh.

YUDE HERSH: Praise God for the bad? Well, you can if you want to. Dear Lord, thank you for slapping me. Lord, thank you for kicking me, for spitting on me. Thank you, oh God, for setting my house on fire. Thank you for visiting a plague upon my livestock. Thank you for chucking my son down a well. Thank you for hanging my wife. Thank you, oh Lord, for decorating my body with screaming boils. Thank you for –

URELE slaps him around the back of the head.

URELE: Thank him for that.

YUDE HERSH: Seriously, though. How can you praise him for good… I mean, for the bad… For the bad? Is that really what the Talmud says, holy Rebe?

ZISHE shrugs.

URELE: It's in the book of Chagiga, chapter six, passage three. It goes 'And we are obliged to praise the Lord for all the bad and for the good as well'…

YUDE HERSH: The answer is in the passage.

URELE: What do you mean?

YUDE HERSH: Because it says, 'we are obliged.'

URELE: But *why*?

YUDE HERSH: Why!

URELE: Why? Please, holy Rebe. I've travelled so far to ask –

YUDE HERSH: Please…

ZISHE: So what you are asking is why are we obliged to praise the Lord for the good as well as for the bad –

URELE: The other way around…

ZISHE: So, why we are obliged –

YUDE HERSH: For the bad!

ZISHE: That's right, to praise God for the bad.

YUDE HERSH: As well as for the good.

ZISHE: *(Bewildered.)* For the bad as well as for the good?

URELE: For the bad as well as for the good. Why, holy Rebe?

ZISHE: Why?

YUDE HERSH: Whywhywhy.

URELE: Why?

Long pause while ZISHE thinks.

ZISHE: I haven't a clue. To be honest… to be honest, nothing bad has ever really happened to me.

Pause.

URELE: I see.

YUDE HERSH: What do you see?

URELE: I think… I understand…

URELE laughs. Suddenly YUDE HERSH jumps up.

YUDE HERSH: Oi, you ahzes ponim! Go bite your mother, why don't you!

He slaps the ants: the other two laugh.

MOYSHELE: Urele spends only a few days in Hanipol. He has to go, but he really enjoyed himself in the company of holy Rebe Reb Zishe. But he still hasn't found his Teacher even here on the anthill.

AVRUMENKO: They just sat there contemplating the psalms sung by the frogs in the cart tracks, scratching to the glory of God.

The sound of frogs and crickets slowly fades out. Long silence.

8
(The Master)

A prayer sung by a nightingale.

Music: the dawn-queen.

Pots rattling. BHABI screeches from the house:

BHABI: Shloymeleeee. Shloymeleeeeee.

A small old man is sleeping under the Sukkah-tent.

BHABI: *(From inside the house.)* Time to get up! Shlomo?
Are you deaf? Get up already, you pitsegepore.

SHLOYMELE: Hedad. You're right, Bhabi: (*Yawns.*) it is not
we that have stepped over the threshold of the new day,
but the new day that has stepped over our threshold – we
must not try to evade it.

He sits up – wearing a nightshirt and a night-time skullcap.

The basin?

BHABI: *(Still inside.)* There's the basin.

SHLOYMELE: There's the basin… but it's too far!

BHABI: You're too far!

SHLOYMELE: Bring it closer.

BHABI: No!

SHLOYMELE: Bring it closer!

BHABI: I don't see why I should. Let the basin come to you.

SHLOYMELE: Hedad! You're right, Bhabi: faith moves
mountains… what's a little basin?

*Looks at the basin, tries to get it to move… The basin tips a
bit, but then falls back.*

SHLOYMELE: The *Shulchan Arukh* book of laws says: 'you must leave the bed as soon as you wake, and you may take at most, four steps to the wash basin…'

Hmmn. Four steps. However… the *Shulchan Arukh* is unclear on how many steps the basin may take…

Thinks.

Well, if the basin will not come to Shloymele, then…

Gets up and takes a large step.

One, for the glory of God!

Takes a bigger step.

Two, for the glory of God!

Takes an even bigger step.

Three. For the glory of God!

Takes an enormous jump.

Fooouuuurrr!

But the basin is still too far away. SHLOYMELE gets down on all fours, then onto his stomach. Finally, at full stretch, he can reach the leg of the kitchen stool, and pulls it carefully towards himself. The basin falls.

BHABI: *(Running onstage.)* Don't strain yourself, do not strain yourself, if I've told you once I've told you a thousand times do not strain yourself!

She stands him upright, takes the kitchen stool over to him, and makes him sit down on it.

SHLOYMELE: *(Crying.)* Bhabi, dearest Bhabi, my life, my sweetest little flower, the basin, please, give me the basin…

BHABI: Alright, alright. You should've asked.

She puts it in his lap, Shloymele performs the ritual cleansing.

BHABI: *(Brings his clothes.)* Will you be wanting lunch?

SHLOYMELE rushes off.

Now where are you running off to?

SHLOYMELE: To the place 'where there is no day and no night...'

BHABI: Ahhhh. Number one?

SHLOYMELE: On the contrary.

BHABI: Number two.

SHLOYMELE: *(Bowing repeatedly to the privy door.)* Praise to you, oh, most glorious guardian angels. Watch over me, protect me! And wait for me, wait for me, while I go inside and come back out again. For this is the necessity of man.

Goes in and closes the door.

BHABI: What do you want for lunch? Can you hear? Kartoflyes? (*Giggling.*) Or would you rather have zhemakes or erdepl? Eh? ... Bulbes? Or should we have a little barbulyes or krumpirn? Or if you really want, if you're very good I can make you a little grechen greplach. Is that what you fancy?

SHLOYMELE: *(Comes out of the privy.)* Hedad!

BHABI: Oh no! I can't make grechen greplach: no buckwheat. Oy, oy. My Lord! Where could I get some buckwheat?

SHLOYMELE: Zhemakes is fine.

He takes off his nightshirt. BHABI dresses him.

BHABI: Or should we have erdepl instead? Or barbulyes? Say something! Are you coming home for lunch or not?

SHLOYMELE: I don't know.

BHABI: What do you mean you don't know?

SHLOYMELE: Bhabi dearest, I don't know if I'm coming home.

BHABI: What do you mean, 'Bhabi dearest, I don't know if I'm coming home'?

SHLOYMELE: Relax, relax…

BHABI: Don't you 'relax, relax' me.

SHLOYMELE: Bhabi, now I'm off to the Prayer House …

BHABI: I know you're going!

SHLOYMELE: And there I will say the great morning prayer, and my soul will hover on the edge of life. Who knows if it will return to this world or not?

BHABI: So you're not coming home for…

SHLOYMELE: Maybe. Maybe yes, maybe no. Maybe my soul will return. But then I will offer myself to the One True Lord, and will sacrifice myself for Him. After saying the great prayer, I will cast myself before the Lord and offer myself to Him once again. Who knows, maybe this time the Lord will accept the offer and will keep my soul. So how can I promise you that I'm going to be home for lunch? Where's my skullcap?

BHABI: On your head.

SHLOYMELE: Where is my shtreimel?

He is now dressed: patent leather-shoes, white stockings, breeches and long silk caftan.

BHABI: I'll get it. *(He runs off, comes back and puts the shtreimel on his head.)* Mazel tov.

SHLOYMELE: Hedad.

He starts to go. URELE is staring from the other side of the gate. Shloymele turns back.

Where is, where is my etrog?

BHABI: Where did you have it last?

SHLOYMELE: Bhabi, please, for the love of God, Bhabi, please...

BHABI: Alright, alright! Don't cry! I'm looking.

SHLOYMELE: What's the point? You're so messy, you just throw things – Here, it is in my pocket. *(Smells the etrog – it is a citrus fruit.)* God bless you.

URELE stops at the gate. YUDE HERSH tries to pull him away but he is rooted to the spot.

SHLOYMELE: Shalom aleichem.

URELE: Al... aleich... aleichem shalom.

BHABI: Shlomo.

SHLOYMELE: Bhabi dear?

BHABI: So are you gonna be home for lunch or not?

Shloymele's voice is heard singing the Hallel prayer in the darkness.

AVRUMENKO: Urele wants to shout, but his tongue is tied. He wants to run after him, but his knees are trembling – he stands and watches as this little old man is swallowed up by this croaking flock now descending upon the Prayer House.

Urele's soul soared! After all these years, after all his travels and suffering – he has found the one for whom he searched!

There is a lulav (palm branch) on the shrine, next to it the etrog.
They recite the Hallel prayer rising in melody and volume.

MOYSHELE: Urele enters – his heart dances with boundless joy. So long, so far, so much hardship… He can now hear the voice of his *Teacher*. But no matter where he looks he can't see him. Not anywhere.

THE GIRL: And then he finds him, where no ordinary person would ever think to look. So endless was the Master's love for the almighty, so great his humility – that he had become embodied into the etrog: he had become one with the fruit.

The little etrog is moving on the altar, crying and shouting the prayer, increasingly ear-splitting and ecstatic.

AVRUMENKO: (*Over the noise.*) And then… the Master is rewarded with that gift that we all long for. During his prayer, when his soul hovers there on the edge of life itself, offered to the Almighty as a sacrifice – the Lord, in his boundless graciousness, finally accepts this offering.

At the height of the prayer, a fat peasant barges in with a baker's shovel.

PEASANT: What do you think you're doing screeching at dawn, shaking your arses at this hour bleating away lie mad sheep? I'm trying to sleep! I want to sleep, for once in my life, I'd like to sleep! Can you hear? Sleep! Sleep! Sleep!

He whacks the etrog with a shovel.
The prayer breaks off.

PEASANT: I just want to sleep. Okay?
Do vidjenia!

Exits.

Shocked pause.

YUDE HERSH: Well... Worse things happen in Judea. Eh?
Am I right?
I'm right...
Am I right?

URELE: You're right.

YUDE HERSH: You see? – Ayse mayse kikele kayse, says
the Talmud: each true Hassid should have two Teachers,
one *living*, and one *dead.* You're a lucky man; you found
both in the same day. And they both fit in your pocket.
(Picks up the flattened etrog.)

URELE: Put it down, and get out of here!

YUDE HERSH: No. I will not.
I too have found my Teacher.

URELE: Where?

YUDE HERSH: In... in Koritz.

URELE: Then go back to him!

YUDE HERSH: What? Oh, you think I mean that Holy
Chochem? That dumbest of the dumb? No, no, no. Don't
you remember? I was standing there, in the main square,
herding my geese –

URELE: I remember you shouting like a –

YUDE HERSH: And my tongue was tied, and my knees
trembled, because you appeared on the road... holy
Rebe...

URELE: What are you talking about?

Pause.

Well, tell me then, what have you learnt from your
Master?

YUDE HERSH: Lots. Lots and lots.

URELE: Like what?

YUDE HERSH: Like…
lots.
Everything.
Shoelaces.

URELE: What?

YUDE HERSH: Like how my Master ties the laces on his boots.

(Takes his boot off.) We hold the laces in our right hand, pass it from our right hand to our left hand, and pass it through the bottom right hole, like so…

URELE: There are great and sublime secrets in the lacing of shoes.

YUDE HERSH: …then we take the lace into our right hand, and pass it through the second left hole across –

URELE: Ayse mayse kikele kayse, have I found a Yude Hersh?

YUDE HERSH: A Yude Hersh. May the Light of my merits protect us!

URELE: Amen

URELE takes the lulav bouqet and the etrog in his hands, finishes off the hallel prayer, lamenting, bending to all four points of the compass. YUDE HERSH copies him, but instead of an etrog holds one of his boots in his hand. Darkness.

9
(Yude Hersh)

SARAH and THE GIRL make beds under the Sukkah-tent. Willow branches and ivy hang down from it, and through the holes of the leafy roof one or two stars peep through.

They are all lying on the straw.

The band plays a tip-cat.

AVRUMENKO: So Urele went home to Lemberg to his wife. She was furious: 'All this searching and what have you found? What? A Yude Hersh!' The once angelic Fraidele had become a hideous nag. She picked at her husband day and night, harassing him for a divorce. These words weighed heavy on Urele's heart. One night he woke her up: 'Look' he said, pointing to the wet pillow. 'What more do you want? Do want your divorce?'

SARAH: Fraidele stopped picking and became quiet. She went from quiet to happy and from happy to loving. And nine months later, a son was born. A wealthy merchant was the witness at the circumcision, Reb Simche Binem.

THE GIRL: And from that moment on, Reb Simche Binem drowned them with gifts. But Urele feared to become wealthy, so one night he loaded Fraidele, the cradle, and Yude Hersh onto a sleigh, and they fled.

MOYSHELE: They glided through the dark forest at night, but Urele felt no fear, for wherever he was, he feared only the Lord Almighty.

AVRUMENKO: And Yude Hersh felt no fear, because he feared only Him, his Teacher who sat next to him in the driver's seat, wearing a sable-fur hat as they passed the pipe between them to warm their hands.

MOYSHELE: And the little donkey pulling the sleigh felt no fear either, for his fearful Master, Yude Hersh, was sitting up there behind him.

THE GIRL: And the baby felt no fear, because he was slumbering in the arms of his Almighty Mother.

SARAH: And Fraidele felt no fear. Fraidele's soul was escaping this world, wandering now in the gardens where the angels lounged in the sun.

MOYSHELE: But suddenly the donkey rears up. A huge bear stands in the middle of the road. Anyone else would have been terrified, but Yude Hersh smiles, gets off the sleigh and the bear comes over to him and kneels. Yude Hersh speaks long and low and the bear listens. Then he skins the bear and puts the fur on Fraidele, who desperately needs the warmth.

THE GIRL: The sleigh continued on its way. The night passed. Morning came bringing nothing but an icy gale howling over the marshes, no sign of a village where they might get some food. And then a flock of doves settles amongst them. They lay their tiny heads on Yude Hersh's knee and beg him with their coos to have their throats slit by his tender hands.

YUDE HERSH takes out his knife.

SARAH: But Fraidele does not see the knife. For in front of Fraidele a pillar of flames leaps up into the sky. And on this pillar of flames little souls climb up into heaven. Hundreds and hundreds of little souls, drawn to the sleigh from far and wide, where Yude Hersh cleanses them with his knife, dresses them in scarlet shirts and sends these innocent little sparks of creation to the eternal redemption.

AVRUMENKO: And Urele harvests icicles from the bushes to make a glowing blaze, and soon from that

Ukrainian snowfield – the celestial smell of roasting
meat drifts towards heaven.

THE GIRL: The sleigh pulled into Strelisk.

MOYSHELE: Strelisk! A small town, covered with snow
above and sunk in swamp below, a place where from
time immemorial the Hassid people trudged through
their lives like geese without a shepherd: *without a rabbi.*

SARAH: This is how holy Urele gained his Kingdom of
Strelisk.

THE GIRL: That is how he became *The Seraph, Holy Reb
Urele of Strelisk.*

AVRUMENKO: Yude Hersh became a shochet. But a
shochet unlike any the world has ever known. Animals
were not afraid of his knife – they longed for it. From far
and wide, from every corner of the globe doves and
geese flocked to Strelisk and into the hands of Yude
Hersh.

MOYSHELE: Once a whole herd of oxen marched from
Moscow to Strelisk.

AVRUMENKO: From Moscow?

MOYSHELE: Alright: Vladivostok. Happy?

SARAH: After Fraidele's death, Urele has married Big
Blime, the daughter of Reb Kopl. And Reb Kopl said:
'Only one thing do I envy my son in law; his disciple,
Yude Hersh. I have never known a Teacher who thinks
more about his disciple. These two are like David and
Jonathan, about whom the Talmud says that they were
like Moses and Joshua, and Moses and Joshua were the
sun and the moon.'

MOYSHELE: That doesn't come close. The holy Seraph
sometimes even sent Yude Hersh on missions to

Hungary! And he said that no one, no one on earth could fully appreciate all that Yude Hersh had accomplished in Hungary. This they will learn of only when the messiah comes.

AVRUMENKO: What did this Yude Hersh accomplish in Hungary?

MOYSHELE: I would tell you, but it's another story. A long story. If I started, by the end of it you'd all've fallen asleep or kicked me out.

AVRUMENKO: Alright. But let's finish this story.

MOYSHELE: Then sleep.

AVRUMENKO: Then sleep.

MOYSHELE: One thing left… in his old age, the holy Seraph went blind. This was a great blessing from God: he no longer had to see the wickedness of the world. He sat in the window, and if he heard footsteps outside, he yelled, 'Look at the vileness of this world!'

THE GIRL: And once, Yude Hersh walked past the window…

YUDE HERSH and a donkey look in the window.

URELE: Look at the vileness of this world!

YUDE HERSH: I'm looking… but I'm not seeing.

URELE: Have you gone blind too?

YUDE HERSH: Just the opposite. Holy Rebe, this world is beautiful.

URELE: Really…

YUDE HERSH: And… brilliant!

URELE: Tell me more.

YUDE HERSH: With words? That isn't possible. It has to be seen to be believed. Anyway, I'm on my way to –

URELE: What's the hurry?

YUDE HERSH: I have to sharpen my knife, and then skin these geese… *(Looks at the audience.)*

URELE: Gitz gepoylt.

YUDE HERSH: Let's go, Talmud.

URELE: Who are you talking to?

YUDE HERSH: Can't see this wise man of mine; Talmud…

URELE: Who is your wise man?

YUDE HERSH: Give me your hand… *(Puts URELE's hand on the donkey.)* … Can you feel? Here are his ears…nose… his furry chin… Oi, Talmud. How many times do I have to tell you not to lick the faces of holy men? For the Talmud says – hey, wait, where are you going? Oi!

Runs after the donkey.

THE GIRL: On the morning of that day, the day that Urele died, he had his phylacteries removed from him and he said:

URELE: 'Today I will be freed from the phylacteries and all the commandments. And I will be free from a Yude Hersh.'

THE GIRL: At night, he sighed:

URELE: 'How beautiful and brilliant this world truly is, if only we do not lose our way – but what an empire of chaos, if one is lost in this world.'

THE GIRL: That was the last thing he said.

MOYSHELE: Didn't he say anything else?

THE GIRL: Sorry?

MOYSHELE: Didn't he say anything else for the last time?

THE GIRL: No.

SARAH: Yes he did.

AVRUMENKO: What did he say?

Pause.

SARAH: He said 'When the messiah comes –'

URELE: When the messiah comes... When the messiah comes, and all the saints go to meet him, in a long-long line, an endless procession: the great Baal Shem Tov, the Great Maggid, Holy Chochem, Wisest of the Wisest of the Wise and all the others – believe me, the one leading the procession will be my Yude Hersh.

SARAH: Then he snickered, chortled, laughed, and giggled and died.

The band plays a short finale.
Silence.
They lie in the Sukkah-tent, sleeping or staring at the sky.
The only sounds are the crickets chirping and the frogs croaking a psalm to the glory of God.

The End